DEVELOPMENT FINANCE COMPANIES:
ASPECTS OF POLICY AND OPERATION

DEVELOPMENT FINANCE COMPANIES:
ASPECTS OF POLICY AND OPERATION

Edited by
William Diamond

Essays by
E. T. Kuiper,
Douglas Gustafson
P. M. Mathew

Published by
THE JOHNS HOPKINS PRESS
for
THE WORLD BANK GROUP

Copyright © 1968 by
The Johns Hopkins Press, Baltimore, Maryland 21218
Manufactured in the United States of America
Library of Congress Catalogue Card Number 68–27738
All Rights Reserved.

CONTENTS

INTRODUCTION		1
1. THE PROMOTIONAL ROLE OF A DEVELOPMENT FINANCE COMPANY—*by E. T. Kuiper*		5
	Introductory Note	5
I.	What Is Promotion?	7
II.	How Does a Promotor Work?	8
III.	Why Should a Development Finance Company Engage in Promotional Activities?	10
IV.	The Elements of Promotion	12
V.	Costs and Risks of Promotion	21
2. PROMOTING BROADER OWNERSHIP OF PRIVATE SECURITIES IN THE LOW INCOME COUNTRIES—*by Douglas Gustafson*		25
	Introductory Note	25
I.	Reasons for Encouraging Widespread Security Ownership in Low Income Countries	27
II.	Factors Chiefly Influencing the Broadening of Securities Markets	28
III.	The Role of the Development Finance Company in Broadening Securities Holdings	32
IV.	Conclusions	46

3. RELATIONSHIP BETWEEN A DEVELOPMENT FINANCE COMPANY AND THE MANAGEMENT OF ENTERPRISES IT PROMOTES, SPONSORS, OR FINANCES—*by E. T. Kuiper* 49

    Introductory Note   49
I. Basic Perspective   51
II. Obtaining Information   53
III. Representation on Boards of Directors   54
IV. Participation in Management?   56
V. Conclusions   58

4. FINANCIAL POLICY PROBLEMS OF DEVELOPMENT FINANCE COMPANIES— *by Douglas Gustafson* 59

    Introductory Note   59
I. Main Elements of the Problem   61
II. Debt-Equity Relationships   64
III. Analysis of the Debt-Equity Problem with the World Bank Model   65
IV. Policies Regarding Reserves and Risk Provision   76
V. The Influence of Taxation on the Financial Policy of Development Institutions   85
VI. Interest Spreads   88
VII. Conclusions   90

5. RELATIONS BETWEEN GOVERNMENTS AND DEVELOPMENT FINANCE COMPANIES— *by P. M. Mathew* 91

    Introductory Note   91
I. Basis for Cooperation   93
II. Public Economic Objectives   94
III. Government Assistance   96
IV. Government Influence   97
V. Government Interference   100
VI. The Government Director   102
VII. Relationship with Public Financial Agencies   103
VIII. Safeguarding Independence   106

APPENDIX
    Participants in the Conference of Development Finance Companies, October 11–13, 1965   109

INDEX 113

DEVELOPMENT FINANCE COMPANIES:
ASPECTS OF POLICY AND OPERATION

INTRODUCTION

In October 1965, the chief executives, or their deputies, of eighteen development finance companies met at the headquarters of the World Bank in Washington. Together with a few staff members and consultants of the International Finance Corporation, they spent three days discussing in depth some of the problems they meet in managing the institutions they head.

This was not the first Conference of Development Finance Companies sponsored by the World Bank Group.[1] The first occurred in May 1958. In the interval of more than seven years, the number of development finance companies financed by the World Bank Group grew from five to twenty-one; its financial involvement in them grew from $43 million to $445 million; the impact of the older of the institutions on the economies of the countries in which they operate became evident and widely acknowledged.

Unlike the 1958 meeting, invitation to the 1965 Conference was limited to the twenty-one companies financed by the World Bank and the IFC.[2] Several of the twenty-one had been promoted by the Bank or the IFC, and bore the imprint of

[1] The International Bank for Reconstruction and Development (IBRD, the World Bank) and its affiliates, the International Development Association (IDA) and the International Finance Corporation (IFC).
[2] By 1967, there were twenty-six of them, and Bank Group financial involvement stood at $675.9 million.

common parenthood; all of them had received some finance from the World Bank Group and consequently had an outlook and a policy congenial to it. As a result, the companies invited, although widely different in many ways, shared a common philosophy and often a common financial structure and policy, which made it easier to sit down together to discuss common problems. The Conference of 1965 was thus a family affair, as the Conference of 1958 was not.

The familial character of the companies, reflected in similarities of outlook, rested on two underlying facts: All of them were established to promote and to finance the expansion of private economic activity; and they were set up as shareholder owned and controlled finance companies. These two facts imposed upon each of the institutions the necessity of operating on the basis of financial, economic and technical criteria rather than on the basis of political criteria. And they imposed the discipline of having to operate in a prudent and profitable way, so as to promise shareholders a reasonable return on their investment. This is a vitally important discipline which, more than any other single factor, is responsible for such success and effectiveness as the institutions have had.

Of the twenty-one institutions invited to the Conference, eighteen came. Four came from Europe (Finland, Spain, Austria, Turkey); four from Africa (Morocco, the Ivory Coast, Liberia, Nigeria); four from Latin America (three from Colombia and one from Venezuela); and six from Asia (China, India, Iran, Israel, Pakistan, the Philippines). Of the eighteen institutions, only three existed when the 1958 Conference took place, and only the Industrial Development Bank of Turkey and the Pakistan Industrial Credit and Investment Corporation participated in it.

The representatives of these institutions were all top executives: Presidents, Vice Presidents, Managing Directors, General Managers or their Deputies. In addition, the four men who were IFC representatives on the Boards of several of the development finance companies participated in the Conference. The level of participation assured a fruitful discussion by persons able to speak authoritatively on the problems and policies of the institutions they represented.

The Agenda of the Conference was drawn up in consultation with the development finance companies and reflected their specific and immediate concerns. It is remarkable, but not surprising, how common those concerns are. Whether in

Finland or in Thailand, in Pakistan, Spain or Colombia, boards and managements struggle with questions involving the promotional and entrepreneurial role of their companies; with the problems of establishing a constructive relationship with the enterprises they promote or finance; with such difficult questions of financial policy as how much to borrow in relation to equity, and how much of profits to pay out as dividends and how much to retain in the company; with the task of resisting governmental pressure, yet being sufficiently responsive to governmental policy to justify the official financial support without which most companies would not have the resources to do their jobs; with developing an effective staff. Not all companies are troubled by all these problems; those that are, are affected to differing extents. Yet the overwhelming majority of them placed these problems, issues, questions, and tasks at, or near, the top of the subjects that cause them the greatest concern.

The discussion was too diverse and too complex to be susceptible to summarization or synthesis, certainly not in a way which would do justice to its range and flavor. Conclusions were not reached. It would, indeed, have been impossible to do so, for the time available was too short to exhaust the flow of ideas, and the subjects were not of the kind where discussion could lead to concrete conclusions. The participants in the Conference did not expect to receive answers to the problems they faced or to the questions they asked; they sought, and I think found, some enlightenment from the experience of others, which could be helpful in finding their own answers and new approaches to their problems.

One clear conclusion did, however, emerge from the Conference. Although there was substantial similarity in the basic problems faced by the eighteen companies, those problems manifested themselves in complex and diverse ways, reflecting the differing size, history, resources, and state of economic development of the sixteen countries in which they were located. The difference in detail, and the widely different environments, suggested that similar problems would have to be dealt with in many varying ways and would find varying solutions from one country to the next. At the very least, the exchange of views on many questions sharpened the questions themselves, suggested options not previously thought of, and thus opened the way to useful solutions tailored to the particular situation of each of the companies represented.

It is not possible, unfortunately, to make available to other development finance companies and to a wider public the experiences laid out and the views expressed at the Conference. It was fundamental to the usefulness of the discussion that the participants speak frankly, and this was possible only in the knowledge that the discussion would be confidential.

In place of "proceedings," there is presented here an essay on each of the subjects discussed at the Conference.[3] Each essay is a personal view, the work of its individual author, reflecting his outlook. Perhaps no participant in the Conference would find himself in full agreement with all the views expressed in the essay. Nevertheless each essay has been written by a person with experience in the work of development finance companies, who participated in the Conference or who observed it, and who has had the opportunity to reflect on the discussion that took place.

All the essayists are associated with the World Bank Group. E. T. Kuiper has been associated with it, in one capacity or another, for a decade and has been involved in investment banking for an even longer time. He has been chief executive of the Industrial Bank of Indonesia, the Pakistan Industrial Credit and Investment Corporation, the Development Bank of Ethiopia, and Malaysian Industrial Development Finance Limited. He has taken on various special assignments for the World Bank Group including representation of IFC on the boards of directors of development finance companies in Greece, Morocco, and Tunisia.

P. M. Mathew became a member of the staff of the IFC in 1962 and was subsequently appointed Deputy Director of the Development Finance Companies Department. Douglas Gustafson is also a staff member of the IFC. Both Mathew and Gustafson have had assignments with development finance companies in Nigeria.

The authors of the essays, and I, are grateful for the careful editing done by Mr. Frank O'Brien, Jr., Chief of IFC Information Services.

William Diamond

Director, Development Finance Companies Department, International Finance Corporation

---

[3] One item on the Agenda, the Training of Personnel and the Use of Expatriate Staff, was not discussed because of shortage of time.

THE PROMOTIONAL ROLE OF A DEVELOPMENT FINANCE COMPANY

by E. T. Kuiper

INTRODUCTORY NOTE

The first subject on the Agenda of the Conference of Development Finance Companies from which the essays in this collection were derived concerned the role of the development finance company in promotional activity. The provision of capital is the hard core of the function of a development finance company. But, should it also help formulate, initiate and organize a proposal for industrial investment? Does it have such an entrepreneurial role to play, as well as a financial one? What are the circumstances and the ways in which a development finance company can appropriately and prudently take the initiative and the leadership in conceiving and fashioning proposals for new enterprises, organizing the finance for them, and carrying them out? What are the costs and risks of such activity?

A variety of views was expressed on these questions, views which tended in general to reflect the level of economic development in the country concerned. Those who were most reluctant to take the lead in promoting enterprises were from countries in which there was already a large and active entrepreneurial class, while those that stressed most vigorously the need for promotional activity came from countries where investment opportunities existed but where entrepreneurs to grasp these opportunities were conspicuously absent or were hard to convince of the merits of new proposals in new fields.

Yet even the managers of companies in the more underdeveloped countries considered that the primary function of their institutions was to provide finance and to organize the provision of finance. There was a general reluctance to take the primary responsibility for the formulation and execution of a project and an awareness of the moral as well as financial risks involved, of the danger of spreading staff capacities too thinly, and of the seductive effects of promotion on staff, which tended to find promotion much more exciting than the more pedestrian activity of appraising the projects of applicants. Some criteria emerged from the discussion, to cope with these risks and dangers. For instance, promotion should be undertaken only in industries which are of national importance and should involve operations which are large enough to make the considerable risks worthwhile.

Mr. N. M. Uquaili, then Managing Director of the Pakistan Industrial Credit and Investment Corporation, and now Finance Minister of Pakistan, chaired the discussion of promotional activity. In summing up his reaction to the discussion, he said that the main functions of development finance companies, with respect to promotion, were to suggest improvements in projects submitted to them for approval, to assist in finding technical and entrepreneurial partners, to assist in finding funds for large projects, to arrange for the preparation both of industrial surveys and of feasibility studies for specific projects, and to make equity investments and carry out underwriting operations and thereby attract other private investors. Since development finance companies were primarily financial institutions, their promotional role had to be limited. But sometimes the objective situation called for promotional activity. The cost should be borne by the sponsors of the project which emerged from the promotion, that is by the new enterprise itself, although such expenses might also be shared by development finance companies, national governments, and friendly foreign governments.

I. WHAT IS PROMOTION?

One of the primary responsibilities of a banker is concern for security and interest margins. He is expected to be conservative and to look with a certain suspicion on untried ideas. A development finance company, on the other hand, must create for itself the image of an activist institution, interested in development and unafraid of change and fully aware that there can be no development without new ideas. This approach involves the development finance company in a variety of activities which may be bundled together under the name of "promotion."

The customary definition of promotional activity by a development finance company involves direct entrepreneurial activity: taking the initiative in shaping up a business and in getting it started.

In looking at applications for finance, a banker will not look only at security and the creditworthiness of the sponsor. He will look primarily at the project, and will try to suggest improvements in it. This is the minimum activity that falls under the name of promotion. At the other end of the spectrum, maximal promotional activity involves a development finance company in a project from its conception; in the extreme case, the development finance company originates the idea, transforms it into a financeable project, perhaps with the help of consultants, arranges the financing, organizes the company and, if only for a time, manages the new enterprise.

Between their minimum and maximum roles, there is a wide range of possibilities, of promotional activities which a development finance company can undertake. Among them are:

    (1) arranging for general industrial surveys and feasibility studies for special projects;

(2) formulating specific proposals for new enterprises;
(3) assisting in finding technical and entrepreneurial partners for local clients or for foreign investors;
(4) investing in share capital and underwriting securities, in order to attract other investors;
(5) arranging mergers, in order to create more economic industrial units;
(6) developing a capital market by trying to broaden ownership and by other devices; and
(7) encouraging the acceptance of new ideas in the economic sector.

Development finance companies are, of course, not the only promotors in the underdeveloped countries. They should always realize that their activities are part of a general urge to change a stagnant situation, and their activities should be coordinated with those of other institutions and individuals (and the government) devoted to the same end.

II. HOW DOES A PROMOTOR WORK?

How does a promotor, whether private individual, development finance company, government agency, or business enterprise, go about "promoting"?

The promotor will first *identify* a project that appeals to him, perhaps the manufacture within the country of an article currently imported or the processing for export of a primary product that presently leaves the country as a raw material. He will next *formulate* the project; he will make studies to establish the economic, financial, and technical feasibility of the venture. The studies must answer the following questions: Can we produce it? Can we sell it? Can we make a profit? If a project of importance is involved, the promotor will—at this crucial stage in the project—almost always have to seek expert assistance. If the venture passes this critical stage of formulation, the promotor may then pass to the phase of *initiation*. In this stage, technical know-how is engaged; partners, agents, and distributors are found; a capital structure is determined; and technical plans are blueprinted. Finally, the project passes to the stage of *execution:* financing is arranged, sites are acquired, tenders are solicited, contracts are closed, machinery is ordered, and so forth.

Whether or not he is aware of it, every entrepreneur goes through these stages in preparing and executing a new venture. And whether or not he is aware of it, every banker, in considering an application, systematizes his investigation along somewhat similar lines.

A development finance company may contribute to the success of a venture at any one of these stages of project development. In the initial stage of identification, it may have a broader or more balanced perspective than the individual entrepreneur can have of the practicability of an idea, or it may be better equipped to carry out a market survey at home or abroad. During the crucial stage of project formulation, the development finance company may have better access, through its international contacts, than the entrepreneur to more reliable information and to expert consultants abroad. Previous experience in project appraisal and international contacts can also be of crucial importance in the more advanced stages of project initiation and execution.

While a development banker will be the first to admit that he has learned much of his business from his client, his client will concede that he owes more than capital to his banker. There is only a thin line between "financing only" and "promotion." For effective appraisal involves a careful scrutiny of each of the factors involved in promotion. Moreover, every project for which financing is sought must be reviewed from the point of view of economic development, because ventures that do not in some way contribute to the growth of the economy will, in a dynamic situation, sooner or later prove to be bad projects from a financial point of view. It is therefore essential that the development banker keep an eye on future prospects in a growing economy. The difference between assuming long-term financial commitments, on the one hand, and promoting, on the other, reflects mainly the development finance company's degree of initiative and the margin of risk it is willing to assume. Of course, it is the profitability of the project itself that determines whether or not a "secured" loan will, in the long run, prove more or less risky than an investment in survey and research or an equity investment. Trust in tangible assets as "security" for loans and for equity is more deeply rooted than justified.

III. WHY SHOULD A DEVELOPMENT FINANCE COMPANY ENGAGE IN PROMOTIONAL ACTIVITIES?

If "promotion" is broadly defined, it will be difficult to find a development finance company that does not engage in some form of promotion. But promotion by development finance companies is a much rarer phenomenon if, as is customary, one regards it as taking the initiative for arranging general industrial or agricultural surveys or feasibility studies for particular projects, formulating the venture itself and capitalizing an enterprise—in short, when the development finance company does not limit itself to stimulating others but itself assumes entrepreneurial functions. When we view promotion in this light, the question should not be "*Why* does a development finance company engage in promotional activities?" but rather "*When* is a development finance company inclined or bound to do so?" Both attitudes appear among development bankers.

One development finance company associated with the World Bank Group was organized after World War II to assist in the rehabilitation of a country with an impressive prewar industrial history, but one that had greatly suffered from the War. This development finance company felt no need to engage in promotion, for the simple reason that the country had an ample supply of entrepreneurial talent and of technical and commercial experience. The company was kept fully engaged in investigating interesting and ready projects, and its principal problems were the recruitment and training of a staff capable of handling applications and finding the capital to satisfy all credit applicants.

Quite different is the case of another development finance company organized in the late fifties in a newly independent country with no industrial experience at all and with a small entrepreneurial class interested mainly in commerce and real estate. This finance company, which had a dynamic management, felt that it must supply the propulsive force. It therefore became the effective promotor, organizing surveys, engaging consultants and preparing projects that, for lack of outside interest, it financed fully or partly and, in many cases, staffed and managed. After some years of such activity, the management of the company justifiably felt that it had done something significant for the country. But the company was now suffering from its excess of zeal, because much of the institution's capital had been invested in the currently unsalable stock of industrial enterprises, some of which will eventually prosper, but others of which may fail. The company is now in the process of reorganization, new capital is being injected and a new policy is being formulated.

Between these extremes there lies a whole range of variations in orientation and approach.

It is interesting to note that the attitudes of the development finance companies associated with the World Bank Group toward promotional activities reflect the stage of economic development of their respective countries. The institutions most reluctant to engage in promotional activities are those in countries with a large and active entrepreneurial class. Although these companies do occasionally inform their clients of promising prospects and advise on project preparation and possible improvements, their preoccupation is not with industrial promotion but rather with finding funds, stimulating the capital market, attracting foreign investment, and strengthening their staffs in order to deal more effectively with their many applications.

The relatively passive role of the development finance companies in the more advanced of the underdeveloped countries is a phase of their history. After all, the largest, most active, and most prosperous development finance companies are located in New York, London, and Paris, where they play a vital role in arranging mergers, attracting international investment, financing the reorganization or modernization of existing enterprises and underwriting. The more economically advanced of the underdeveloped countries will in due course mature and their institutional structure will grow. As this happens, their development finance companies, which now concentrate on medium- and long-term lending and are reluctant to enter the promotional field, will begin to follow with increasing enthusiasm the patterns of activity of their counterparts in Europe and the United States. On the other hand, it is the development finance companies of countries with a shortage of entrepreneurs that stress the need for and the rewards from promotional activity. They rightly believe that, although they may have a sizable lending business, their countries have opportunities which neither local nor foreign businessmen are grasping. And they consider that one of their legitimate functions is to step into the breach. In doing so, they face many problems.

IV. THE ELEMENTS OF PROMOTION

The Starting Place—Ideas

Although the general public usually regards development finance companies primarily as sources of *financing*, those who sponsor the establishment of such institutions—and national governments are prominent among the sponsors—are often convinced that it is *developmental* activities that should be stressed. Whatever the thought of the sponsors, the managements of development finance companies are inclined to feel that promotion is perhaps the most important, certainly the most difficult, and often the most costly of all their operations.

There are, however, a number of so-called promotional activities that do not, in fact, involve a company in risk and may, for a time, have little direct effect on the profit and loss account. Such activities involve ideas—proposing new ideas.

All promoting starts with an idea. If a development finance company is development-oriented, it will constantly be coming up with new ideas. Such an orientation is more important for the success of a development finance company than the amount of capital at its disposal. For if a development finance company combines a dynamic approach with sound judgment and persistent endeavor, the necessary capital is likely, in the long run, to be forthcoming provided, of course, that the opportunities for investment exist and that the political climate is favorable for economic growth.

Usable Types of Ideas

Ideas for development may vary widely, and may be oriented toward government as well as toward private initiative. Once a development finance company has reached some conclusions about the appropriate direction for national economic development, it may approach the government with suggestions for projects that might be incorporated into the national plan or, if they are already in the plan, might be given a higher priority. Or it may come up with ideas on a more effective orientation of investment policy. It is true that many privately managed development finance companies have not found governmental planning authorities very receptive to their suggestions. Yet the counsel of others has been sought by governments on questions of investment codes, taxation, foreign exchange allotments, and various financial matters; and unsolicited advice has sometimes been well received. There are no two countries in which the relationship between the government and a privately managed development finance company is identical. As will be noted in a later essay, a developmental orientation and successful operation are bound to result, sooner or later, in a fruitful and effective reciprocal relationship.

The Key Move—Bringing Idea and Entrepreneur Together

The real test, however, of the development finance company's effectiveness as a promotor of ideas lies in its contacts with private entrepreneurs, both foreign and domestic. Close and continuing contact with the private business community is crucial. A development banker who does not meet frequently with the community he serves is not in business; a man without ideas for economic growth should not be the executive of a development finance company.

Through its day-to-day contact with the business community, a development finance company can make its knowledge and experience available to others, and bring them to bear on the investment proposals of others. A development finance company with good international connections is in a particularly advantageous position to bring the experience of other countries to bear upon the local situation. Since most development finance companies are located in countries which are relatively stagnant economically because of their traditional orientation to agriculture and to trade, the primary need is often not for its capital, but for its ideas and for the new techniques of production and sales to which it can open its clients' minds.

A development finance company can help bring men who have new ideas or technical knowledge together with men who have capital; the two are not always found together. The function of negotiating such a marriage is particularly important in bringing foreign and domestic businessmen together. A development finance company should have a sound knowledge of the capabilities and limitations of various industries, in relation to their market prospects. It may thus be in a favorable position to promote cooperation, coordination, and mergers among enterprises in the same field, in order to take advantage of opportunities and situations of which the individual entrepreneur may not be aware, with advantage to the economy of the country. The only limit to the possibilities of a development finance company to promote new ideas is the availability of businessmen who can listen intelligently.

Liaison between the Officials and Private Sectors

A development finance company can also act naturally and effectively as a liaison between the government generally and the national planning authorities in particular, on the one hand, and the investing community, on the other. The company can play an essentially pragmatic and common-sense role, choosing between projects that can be implemented at once because their profitability is assured and projects whose execution must be deferred until the economic situation evolves. In helping to coordinate the studies of the planning authorities with the decisions of businessmen, and to make the studies objective as well as realistic, and to relate the investment decisions to general economic objectives, the development finance company plays a critical role.

Development finance companies can act as a link between the entrepreneurial class and the planners by translating the planners' ideas into the concrete specifics required by the entrepreneurs and into a language the entrepreneurs understand. They are strategically placed to undertake this kind of promotional activity; this may well prove the most fruitful branch of the promotional tree for development finance companies.

It should be noted again that none of these activities engages the finance of a development finance company. They engage, rather, its philosophy and the time of its management and staff. Development finance companies that cannot yet invest any funds in equity investment or do not yet have a margin of income for expenditure on surveys and research, can nevertheless be active and effective in influencing others, both government and private businessmen.

Steps from Idea to Investment of Capital

Promotion starts with the generation of ideas. It would be naïve to think, however, that the catalytic function of a development finance company will go very far if the company is not prepared or is not in a position to back ideas with capital. The capital need not be its own. The development finance companies associated with the World Bank Group have had a variety of experiences in putting up and in finding capital to support the ideas they have germinated.

Consultation and Study. If initial inquiries regarding the idea for a project suggest that systematic investigation will lead to concrete results, the development finance company must hire consultants to survey the field or to help formulate a specific financeable proposal—or drop the matter without further ado. Good consultants are neither cheap nor easy to find. A company's foreign and international shareholders and creditors, both of which are usually deeply interested in the welfare of the company, will be able to help find appropriate expertise. In some countries, governments have established funds to finance industrial surveys or project studies, to which development finance companies may have access. It has often also been possible to obtain grants from foreign governments, international agencies, foreign foundations and universities.

Because the development finance company is a profit-oriented institution, it can rarely afford to contribute substantially to such studies, even though it may have initiated them. It will be able, and prepared, to do so only if it can clearly visualize the prospect of recovering its outlay later on, in the process of executing the project. Such a prospect is more likely if the study or survey is narrowly focused. A general economic survey is the least likely to pay off; a study of a specific project is the most hopeful. A survey of a range of projects in a particular field (such as the cement or sugar industry, wood-processing, or mechanical industry) falls somewhere between. The narrower the focus of a study, the more precisely directed it is to a specific project or to a clear-cut group of such projects, the better the possibility that a development finance company can usefully contribute to it from its specialized experience or from its financial resources. So restricted outlays for research and study can sometimes prove fruitful and profitable, and in the process create attractive new investment possibilities and business clients for the development finance company.

Some Latin American development finance companies have sponsored "study funds." They have formed groups with other financiers and industrialists (especially foreign ones) for further study of a specific project or of an entire sector.

The study group (or "promotion company," as it is often called) retains consultants and receives and considers all the pertinent information. If the studies are favorable, the members of the group either finance and carry out the project themselves, or sell the studies at a profit. In either case, the development finance company will have created a client.

It is characteristic of less developed countries that natural resources are insufficiently mapped and that possibilities for their exploitation and marketing have not been properly explored. Governments have the primary responsibility in this sector. Although many planning authorities make such studies with enthusiasm and diligence, they are rather general in character. The business community is occasionally disappointed with the results because it fails to find in "the plan" answers to its practical problems. This is not surprising, for planners must deal at a fairly general level and cannot readily put themselves in the position of the entrepreneur who must risk his capital on the basis of his assessment of a market.

When to Promote New Companies. Development bankers would generally be content to restrict their promotion to the activities discussed thus far: advising, suggesting, helping locate technical and financial partners, arranging for general surveys and for the study of specific projects. Such a posture would enable a development finance company to exercise a helpful influence on the economy as a whole and on the company's applicants in particular, with benefit to the company's loan portfolio and without much financial risk. As a rule, however, such an attitude succeeds only in an environment that is well supplied with private entrepreneurial talent or in which the development finance company enjoys a virtual monopoly in the supply of foreign exchange for long-term capital investment in private industry. Such a situation, however, does not always exist. Where there is not a plentiful supply of entrepreneurs working to exploit investment opportunities and seeking capital to finance them and where the development finance company has no special advantages over competitive institutions, it must sooner or later wet its feet in the treacherous waters of company promotion.

The same may also be true of development finance companies more advantageously placed. One development finance company, which has had fifteen years of operation in a country with a good entrepreneurial environment and which has always had a position of strength in the financial field, has called attention to a cyclical movement in its promotional activities. During boom periods, it received so many applications for financing apparently viable projects that it could not afford to spend time on promotion and found little need to do so. But in periods of relative depression, applications for loans fell substantially; and the company took up old files on development projects and opened new investigations. This company found that, in normal times and on the average, 10 per cent of staff time was devoted to promoting new companies but that in slack times there was no such limit to the efforts staff could devote to such activities.

Other development finance companies, which feel unable to study new projects in present conditions of demand for their finance, may note this experience. A development finance company requires a skilled and experienced staff. It would be regrettable if this asset, created with so much difficulty and expense, were not kept in effective use in slack times.

Company promotion may be particularly important where a development finance company is not in a monopoly position. Some countries have several such companies. Often they are sponsors or co-sponsors of most of the important new undertakings in the countries concerned. There is a danger that not all may find sufficient business to build a sound organization and to make a profit. Yet, generally speaking, there is room in a developing country for all promotion-oriented financial institutions that prove themselves efficient; some competition among development finance companies so oriented stimulates industrial activity.

Ways and Means of Promoting New Companies. The classical approach is for a development finance company to begin with ordinary medium- and long-term loans. As its work proceeds, it considers other ways of financing, such as by convertible loans or debentures or equity investments. It then advances to the more complex forms of promotional activity, such as promoting companies independently. As the staff becomes more experienced and as the portfolio of the development finance company is seasoned, there will be a more solid base for promotional work. In the newly emerging countries, however, many development finance companies cannot follow this classical pattern. The sponsors of the company may have been correct in assuming that there were favorable development opportunities and the company would have a capable staff. Nevertheless the flow of applications may be disappointing in the first years; in such circumstances, one must promote through "pump-priming." Unless the sponsors of the development finance company have made a serious mistake, there will be projects that can be studied by the staff; instead of learning from clients who have not appeared, the staff will learn its business by trial and error and through contacts with more experienced foreign companies.

It should be borne in mind that promotion is a long-term activity; many ideas and only partly studied investment possibilities may be restudied in the light of new developments, as chances for attracting financing appear to have improved, or as the staff has more time to devote to the projects being promoted, rather than to those being offered.

It is a good rule for a development finance company that service to clients should normally take precedence over the company's own promotional activities and that when sufficiently knowledgeable businessmen show an interest in a project that has been promoted by the company for its own account, the company should share its findings with these entrepreneurs. Yet even development finance companies that follow this admirable counsel of self-denial cannot expect always to escape the charge that they are competing with the business community and neglecting the interests of their clients when they themselves take up promotional activities. In addition, in every country there are business and political groups that resent any promotional activity by a development finance company because they suspect that funds and attention are being diverted from matters which interest them. Conversely, for example, in an ex-colonial country, one development finance company with overseas shareholders felt impelled to take the initiative in promoting new industrial ventures in order to dispel the impression that the company was a foreign organization.

When promoting new enterprises for their own account, development finance companies differ in one vital respect from the private entrepreneur. The individual businessman usually intends that he or his group shall own and control the venture for a long time to come, whereas development finance companies have no desire to create enterprises that they must control; they expect to divest themselves of ownership and control in due course and at a profit commensurate with the initial work and risk as well as with the performance and outlook of the enterprise created.

The role of a development finance company in stimulating the capital market will be discussed elsewhere. Suffice it to say here that the same type of activity may be required, and crucial, in company promotion.

The development finance companies that operate in countries in which a capital market already exists or is in the process of developing, find that they can assist in floating new industrial ventures by underwriting part of the share capital required for offering on the stock exchange. This, of course, can be done only when the development finance company is thoroughly acquainted with the project and is confident of its ultimate success. Thus, the development finance company becomes both a partner in the promotion and a co-sponsor of the project. In view of the thinness of the capital market in underdeveloped countries, a development finance company engaging in an underwriting should be prepared to become a substantial investor; for it is more likely than not to be made to sell all of the securities it underwrites. A somewhat similar role is played by the financial institution that forms a syndicate or finds equity capital privately for a new venture; many development finance companies in developing countries perform a useful function in this manner. The exercise need not be limited to equity; the development finance company may prepare an overall financial plan and use its connections and specialized knowledge to arrange a package deal to provide all the finance required for the project, in whatever form.

Foreign investors, as well as national governments, usually prefer a form of joint enterprise in which part of the equity is owned by nationals of the country in which the venture will operate. At the inception of a project, it is often difficult to interest local owners of capital; in these circumstances, a development finance company may, for some time, fill the gap. This has the added advantage of giving the foreign investor confidence that, during the sometimes difficult early years of his enterprise, his partner is not an uncertain and perhaps impatient group of individuals, but is rather a far-sighted institution of prestige.

In any group promotion, there is bound to develop among the partners a division of functions. Thus the technically more knowledgeable assume responsibility for ordering and installing machinery, commercial people prepare markets, while the development finance company draws up budgets, calculates costs, prices, and cash flow, arranges financing and probably, in the end, underwrites not only medium- and long-term loans, but also a substantial part of the equity risk. In several countries, the government has put a substantial amount of money under the management of privately-owned and -managed development finance companies in the form of an "equity fund"; equity participations in enterprises sponsored by the development finance companies are, in part, financed from these funds. This may prove a very sound procedure and one of the best devices for a government that wants to stimulate economic growth and has decided against an increase in government-owned and government-managed enterprises. In many countries, as experience grows and as the private sector becomes more competent and sophisticated, the policy of government has gradually shifted away from the wish to do everything itself and towards indicative planning and policy control, and towards encouraging private enterprise to carry out specific actual projects. Development finance companies may be instrumental in instigating this change in attitude and can offer their services in the process.

Requisites for Promoting New Companies. The extent to which a development finance company may assume the functions that are normally those of the individual entrepreneur depends on two factors, apart from the entrepreneurial environment and the presence of potential projects: capital structure and staff. So far as capital structure is concerned, promotion cannot prudently be carried out with borrowed funds. A substantial equity, and a willingness to wait for a return on it, are vital if company promotion is to loom significantly in the activity of a development finance company. On the staff side, a development finance company will have to attract for its management and senior positions people who combine the alertness of the promotor with a prudent approach to commercial and financial problems. Common sense and the wit to recognize what one does not know are more important for the financier than specialized knowledge. If a development finance company cannot attract a few people with these characteristics, it would be wise to abstain from the more advanced and risky promotional activities.

And if it can find such people, there is another type of risk. One of the dangers of promotion for a development finance company is that both management and staff may begin to find such satisfaction in promotional work that they may become overly involved. This may result in their doing too many promotional jobs, in a relative loss of objectivity, or in their favoring "pet projects," with possible adverse effects on the soundness of the ventures and consequent risks to the reputation of the development finance company. Experience suggests that the best way to avoid the danger of over-involvement is to associate others in the preparation and the execution of projects as soon as practicable.

V. COSTS AND RISKS OF PROMOTION

In the long run, the success or failure of the promotional efforts of a development finance company will be judged by its own Profit and Loss Account and its own Balance Sheet. There should be no misunderstanding about this. No development finance company strives to maximize its profits only in order to pay large dividends to shareholders or large bonuses for its directors. Since the lack of capital is one of the main impediments on the road to economic development, a loss of capital resources is always detrimental to progress. Financial institutions that cannot build up reserves, cannot declare reasonable dividends and cannot show promising profit prospects for the future, will be unable to attract capital and will therefore fail to pull their weight in the march forward. The crux of the matter is that development finance companies must try to combine profit-making with a developmental orientation.

The simple fact is that promotion is both costly and risky, and the management of a development finance company engaged in promotion must keep an ever-vigilant eye on both the costs and the risks.

The costs of promotion are, first, the salaries of personnel devoted to promotional work, plus part of the salaries of the executive staff, general office expenses, etc., and, secondly, out-of-pocket expenses for services supplied by consultants, travel, laboratory research, etc.

The costs of personnel are partly hidden and may therefore be higher than the development finance company realizes. Even if the project promoted is successful, it is often difficult to recover these costs from the sponsors who carry out the venture. But the older and more experienced development finance companies have learned they may not do too much work on a scheme unless they are confident that they will ultimately receive a fair return from the exercise, in the form of a profitable loan operation, underwriting commissions or an equity participation.

The costs of outside services can be more easily ascertained. They can readily be passed on in full to the client of the development finance company or, in the case of a new promotion, to the new company.

Many development finance companies receive substantial support in both categories of expense from their governments and sometimes from foreign aid funds. One such company associated with the World Bank Group receives an annual grant from its government to cover a major portion of the salaries of specialized staff devoted to promotion. In general, such arrangements have worked fairly well and the governments have not attempted to exert undue influence on the type of study undertaken or on the choice of entrepreneur for project implementation.

The costs of study and research may often run into high figures. But while the project is still under study, losses can be cut in time if the promotion shows no promise, and financial involvement may be limited if there is danger that the amount budgeted for the study will be exceeded. All the same, more than one development finance company has incurred losses in dead-end studies and has learned from the experience.

The major financial consequences of a promotion, whether favorable or unfavorable, derive not from the studies undertaken but from the equity investment in the project which the development finance company has decided to back. This is the real risk, even if the equity investment is camouflaged as a "secured loan." (In the case of a new enterprise, sponsored by persons new to the industrial field, there may be little difference between an investment in share capital and an investment in the form of a loan.) But such risks must be taken. They can be avoided, and should be, if studies backed up by business judgment suggest that the risks are not justified, but if everything has been done to establish and to strengthen the inherent soundness of a project, a development finance company may be more to blame for not showing the courage of its conviction than for taking a well-considered equity risk.

Taking such risks does not mean ignoring their existence. Most development finance companies have adopted policies to limit the size of each such equity risk (to a given percentage of net worth) and to limit their aggregate total (to net worth itself). Such a restriction helps safeguard the liquidity and viability of the development finance company. There may be justification for feeling that such investments in equity will, in due course, be profitable; but the time that is likely to elapse before dividends are paid and shares can be sold may exceed the period for which the participating development finance company can afford to forego the income and lock up funds. Another useful device for restricting commitments is to avoid taking a controlling position in an enterprise. Such a posture could well result in additional financial exposure and certainly have the effect of taking up management time.

The greatest non-financial risk of promotion is over-involvement, which has already been referred to. There is a conceptual parallel between financial liquidity on the one hand and, on the other, staff objectivity and flexibility. "Pet projects" often go wrong. Over-devotion to promotions may result in under-devotion to clients. Both may result in loss of the respect and confidence of the business community—without which a development finance company cannot survive. One manager of a development finance company associated with the World Bank family has said that the promotional action which caused him the greatest concern was the sale to the general public of shares in ventures he had promoted, without being able to guarantee that the shares would be profitable or that they would remain in strong and sympathetic hands. His personal sensitivity on these crucial issues was a more effective caution against the risks of promotion than any formal policy declaration could provide.

In general, there seems little doubt that in promotion one may incur considerable losses not only for a development finance company but also for its partners and for the public which it has enticed into investment. It is encouraging, however, that practically all the development finance companies associated with the World Bank Group have thus far avoided most of the pitfalls, and some have done fairly well in the field and are confident of their ability to expand these operations in the future.

2

PROMOTING BROADER OWNERSHIP OF PRIVATE SECURITIES IN THE LOW INCOME COUNTRIES

by Douglas Gustafson

INTRODUCTORY NOTE

Nearly all the development finance companies associated with the World Bank Group have the objectives of promoting the broader ownership of enterprise by encouraging the distribution of private securities. They are supposed to stimulate the growth of the capital market in the countries in which they operate: to find ways of mobilizing savings, to facilitate the flow of those savings by devising types of securities which will be both suitable to the enterprise that needs financing and at the same time attractive to the investor who has the savings, and by encouraging the investor to transform his savings into those securities.

Mr. James Raj, then General Manager of the Nigerian Industrial Development Bank and now Vice President of IFC, led the discussion on this subject. He organized the discussion under four broad headings.

The first was the subject of developing institutional arrangements needed for the growth of a capital market. There must be some method and marketplace for buying and selling before security ownership can be expanded to any significant extent. The second problem to be faced was that of developing different types of securities to fit the particular conditions of the country. This depended on the demand and supply of funds and the requirements of investors; various types of securities needed to be designed to fit their specific needs. The third problem was that of developing an orderly market for securities in order to build public confidence in their ownership. This related to assuring reasonable stability in the market, once shares are widely distributed. The fourth problem concerned the participation of development finance companies in these activities without undue risk. This involved the question of the role of development finance companies in underwriting.

Mr. Raj identified several points on which there seemed to be general agreement among participants at the meeting:

—First, before wide distribution of stocks and expanding ownership was possible, there must be a basic company law, acceptable and qualified accounting, honesty in public disclosures and so forth, which existed in the more developed countries. It was generally felt that development finance companies could play a useful role, if only by requiring such standards from their own clients.

—The second point was that, before a wide capital market could be established, the government's monetary and fiscal measures must be regarded as avoiding hyperinflation. Once the individual investor developed confidence in the value of his money, liquidity and debt instruments suited to the particular environment could be developed.

—A third matter concerned competition between government and private enterprise for funds in the capital market. In some countries, there was a question as to how far the government was prepared to tolerate competition from private enterprise for funds which the government wanted.

—A final point of agreement, and a vital one, was that in helping to maintain an orderly market, a development finance company must not go against the market. There was a case for making a market and, to some extent, being a buyer or seller of last resort, but there was not a case for supporting prices.

I. REASONS FOR ENCOURAGING WIDESPREAD SECURITY OWNERSHIP IN LOW INCOME COUNTRIES

The development finance companies associated with the World Bank Group are expected to make an important contribution to the development of capital markets in the low income countries. To give this objective concrete meaning in a specific environment, three questions need to be answered. Why should the widespread ownership of securities be encouraged? What are the factors chiefly influencing the spread of securities ownership? What is the role of a development finance company in the realization of this objective? The latter two questions are considered under succeeding headings.

First, as to why the spread of security ownership should be encouraged, it may be of economic importance to open up new investment possibilities for the savings of the community. Investment capital is a critical component of economic growth and if the availability of industrial securities means that capital can be mobilized and diverted from less productive investment in such things as real estate into more productive investment in industrial assets, the economy will be better served. In the absence of publicly held securities, the only alternatives for mobilizing and channeling savings into productive investment are by way of the banking system or by the government's gaining access to savings by means of taxation, and investing them in industry. If, however, decentralization of the ownership of assets and a healthy private sector are also objectives, then it is imperative to encourage the widespread ownership of securities and the growth of a capital market. If avoidance of an excessive concentration of power in the hands of the government is an objective, a related goal will no doubt be the avoidance of the concentration of wealth and economic power in the hands of a small private group. The only alternative to these two extremes is widespread individual ownership of assets.

A similar problem may arise in an agrarian society where the equivalent to securities is land ownership. If land is controlled by relatively few people, attaining a more equitable distribution of it will be an important policy matter. In a country that is undergoing some degree of industrialization (even if land ownership is broadly based), as commercial enterprise and industry become more important, citizens will find themselves unable individually to own and control industries as easily as they might be able to own land. Their only way of participating in the ownership or control and in the returns from industry will be through the ownership of industrial securities. Widespread security ownership by individuals or by the institutions to which they have entrusted their savings is thus basic to a reasonable distribution of wealth, income and power.

In countries where foreign enterprises play an important role in industrial development, widespread participation in the ownership of industry may be even more important politically than in countries where industry is controlled by strong local groups. A foreign presence always has some negative aspects, either materially or psychologically, and this becomes more critical as the visibility of the foreign sector increases along with its control of a country's industry. An effective way to deal with this problem, from the viewpoints both of the foreign investor and the local community, is for the foreign concern to open its ownership to participation by private local individuals and institutions. Such a move may be important not only in mobilizing savings for productive investment and achieving a more equitable distribution of wealth, but also in facilitating cooperation between foreign investors and the local community. In fact, the favorable impression created by such a move and the fact that it may result in better cooperation between the parties involved, may be the most important benefit to foreign investors who offer shares of their overseas subsidiaries to local investors.

Unless such objectives as these are accepted in a country, there will be no basic reason or motivation for stimulating the widespread ownership of securities; and a development finance company will find it difficult, if not impossible, to make any progress in this direction.

II. FACTORS CHIEFLY INFLUENCING THE BROADENING OF SECURITIES MARKETS

In countries where securities ownership is not common, a development finance company's role in promoting such ownership will be affected, and may be determined, by the characteristics of the environment in which the company operates. The extent to which the company can deal successfully with these difficulties depends upon the skills of its management as reflected in the company's stature and influence in the community. In some countries, it may be the acknowledged and accepted leader in promoting a local capital market, whereas in others, its influence may be smaller due to the existence of other private or public agencies engaged in the same task. Because development of a capital market is a difficult area of operations, it may be given a low priority; but because of the challenges it offers, a development finance company's contribution in this field can be very important to the economy as well as rewarding to its shareholders and management.

Return on the Investment

The basic condition that must be met if the ownership of securities is to be popularized is that the financial returns must be attractive to the potential investors, taking into account considerations of risk, relative to other forms of investment in the community (or even returns from investments abroad, if investors are accustomed to sending their savings overseas). Often land speculation and investment in commerce are not only the more familiar forms of investment but also the more profitable types of investment. As long as this condition exists, in actuality or in investors' minds, it will be difficult to market industrial securities. Of importance here is how the existing or potential investor evaluates investment alternatives. Is he interested in assured income streams or in capital appreciation? Does he need visible evidence of ownership in real assets as opposed to a "piece of paper"? How important is liquidity? These factors will affect the type of security that will be marketable and the nature, form, and methods of communication by the company to its shareholders. Innovation in security types and marketing procedures will often be required to generate investor interest.

In some cases, legal restrictions may not permit the form of security that appears to be the most suitable for a given situation. If, for example, investors require an immediate return on an investment, a straight equity issue by a new company will not be very attractive, and a possible alternative would be a convertible debenture that has a fixed income combined with an option to convert at a later date into ordinary shares at a specific price. The legal status of convertible debentures may, however, be in doubt, or they may not be permitted. If securities are to be sold, they must fit local requirements, and this may require modifications of the law.

Of course, a basic influence on the returns accruing to investors holding industrial securities will be the nature and performance of the economy, and it is unlikely that a development finance company will be able to affect this directly, although it can be influential in pressing for changes in policies if such changes appear to be necessary and realistic. A high rate of inflation can curb any interest on the part of the public in investing in securities, particularly those with a fixed income. This problem is out of the hands of the development finance company, but the company must take inflationary factors into consideration when it designs security types and when it makes recommendations to investors. Apart from inflation, a tight money market may make it impossible to sell securities when the promise of a reasonable return is in the distant future or when the long-term return is unattractive relative to other forms of investment. In a number of countries, widespread use of consumer financing in a tight money situation may result in high yields on finance company paper, out-stripping all other available yields and thereby channeling a sizable proportion of investable funds into consumer finance at the expense of investment in industry.

Tax Policies

Tax policies affect the popularity and form of security ownership. This is another point at which a development finance company may be able to exert some influence. Of particular importance are the regulations affecting institutional investors such as insurance companies, private pension funds, and government provident funds. In many countries, these institutions may be fairly well developed while the capital market, as far as industrial securities are concerned, is in its infancy. As a result, these investors often represent the most important market for securities, although there may be impediments in the form of tax and legal restraints on their investments, particularly in equities. Also they may not be familiar with new types of investments and the seller of industrial securities may have to educate them.

Taxation is also a very important factor in the investment decisions of individuals. In a number of countries, governments are hard pressed for funds and in order to attract savings the interest rates and tax features of government securities are designed to give them a competitive edge over private securities. The taxation of capital gains relative to normal income is also an important determinant of investors' attitudes.

Even if all these conditions are such as to make investment in the securities of private concerns relatively attractive at the initial stages of security ownership, a very large educational effort may be required, first to inform investors of these new alternatives and then to convince them that they are really suitable. This is a long process. But if the institutions promoting widespread security ownership do an effective job, the response can be surprisingly great, even in very unsophisticated capital markets.

Institutional Facilities

Another vital requirement for the development of widespread ownership of industrial securities is the existence of some type of orderly market for trading in securities. Investors are unlikely to tie up their funds in an investment if there is considerable uncertainty about their ability to liquidate their investment. It is, of course, true that two individuals can make a market; but unless there is some specific place where buyers can, in effect, meet sellers, the development of the capital market will be restricted. Without a marketplace for trading and price determination, each individual must act as his own agent and the market in private securities will be chaotic. Because of the considerable differences in knowledge, sophistication and ethics among the individuals in any community, some form of controlled market, with competitive selling and buying, is necessary if fraudulent transactions are to be avoided and investment in industrial securities is to be encouraged.

Prevailing Business Practices and Ethics

Perhaps one of the most important considerations in broadening a securities market is the business practices and ethics of a society and their influence on security ownership. Where public accountability is lacking it is unlikely that individuals will become minority shareholders in firms, simply because they will not know what is going on inside the company and they will not trust the major shareholder. Consequently, it is often foreign enterprises, which are accustomed to high auditing and accounting standards and to public disclosure, that first offer their securities successfully to the public in countries where security ownership is relatively new. They may be motivated by a government requirement for a local ownership component of foreign firms, a desire to raise capital, a gesture to indicate their willingness to identify themselves with the interests of the local community, or a combination of these. Whatever the motivation, their issues often serve as a starter for security ownership and provide useful examples for local firms to follow.

In many countries the local business community is composed primarily of family concerns, which is the typical business organization in a traditional economy. In such cases, financial data are usually closely guarded against outsiders, including the tax collector. In fact, bookkeeping and accounting procedures and standards within the enterprise may be so fragmentary that even insiders may not know exactly the state of a firm's financial condition and performance. Where this is the accepted pattern of business operation, there will be a strong prejudice against widespread ownership of a company and disclosure of important financial data outside the family group. Potential investors will in such circumstances be wary of putting their money where they do not directly oversee the operation and where their control is diluted. Absentee ownership may not be readily acceptable. Auditing of accounts may be unknown, or at best inaccurate, and there may not be a local accounting profession that can be relied upon. Even if competent local or foreign accounting services are available, it may be difficult to persuade local businessmen to subject their operations to such scrutiny.

III. THE ROLE OF THE DEVELOPMENT FINANCE COMPANY IN BROADENING SECURITIES HOLDINGS

In countries where there is little or no market for securities, it is likely that a development finance company will be in a unique position to take the lead in the development of a capital market. Often these development finance companies are established with international cooperation and thus have access to a significant pool of experience; they are operated in accord with high financial standards; their staffs represent unique sources of knowledge as far as industrial development in their respective countries is concerned; and they often assume a stature of some importance in the private and public sectors of their countries. The facilitation of industrial development will almost always, by definition, include the promotion of the widespread ownership of industrial securities; and most managements of development finance companies consider this as an important area in which their companies can be active and can have a significant influence on the developmental process.

Marketing Its Own Shares and Debentures

Sometimes it is expected that the sale of a development finance company's own securities will be helpful in activating a capital market. To date, however, this intermediary role has not been an important one for most of the development finance companies associated with the World Bank Group. With the exception of Banco del Desarrollo Económico Español (BANDESCO), which has raised most of its resources directly from the public through its own debentures, the companies have raised the bulk of their funds through international lending agencies, through their national governments, or a combination of the two.

National savings are often channeled to the private sector by means of government loans to development finance companies, but this mechanism does not increase security ownership by individuals and private companies, nor does it stimulate a more active capital market.

Although public sale of the shares or debentures of development finance companies has not yet been a common device for promoting the development of a securities market, it could become one in the future, for the more mature development finance companies. Their progress in this area will depend on the volume of savings available, on the willingness of governments to allow these institutions to raise funds locally, and on the attractiveness of the securities offered in relation to alternative investment opportunities.

Nevertheless, even for relatively young companies operating in countries where public interest in security ownership is new, there are several areas in which the companies can make an effective contribution to broadening the securities market. One is in the general upgrading of business and financial practices. Another is in developing a mechanism, if none exists, for effective marketing and trading in securities or improving the existing mechanism. A third is by expanding the number of private securities available for public subscription and trading. Fourth—a matter in which development finance companies can often have a direct hand—is the possibility of expanding the number of institutions and individuals interested in investing in securities. Finally, there may be some situations in which development finance companies can play a very carefully limited and cautious role in helping to maintain an orderly market for securities. The extent to which any of these roles is practicable depends upon the institutional and economic environment. It would be unusual if an effective development finance company did not have a contribution to make in at least one of these areas.

Upgrading Business Practices

A development finance company can have a direct hand in correcting business practices that inhibit public ownership of securities.

First, by setting high standards of performance in its own operations—for instance, by observing high standards of accounting, by observing thorough control procedures, and by making meaningful reports available to its shareholders and the public—it can serve as a model.

Second, as it works closely with its clients both at the appraisal and follow-up stages, the company will be able to educate and influence its clients to upgrade their practices, though this may prove a long-range undertaking. There is, here, the danger that the development finance company may become too rigid in its requirements and frighten business off; if this happens, no one benefits. Thus, judgment is required as to the speed with which it should press for changes in a client's operations and procedures. Sometimes the development finance company will be able to make a start toward upgrading business practices by imposing auditing and reporting requirements on its clients. It may also perform a service by encouraging, or perhaps requiring, clients to use corporate forms of business organization.

A development finance company can assist in upgrading accounting practices, first by example, and then by supporting accounting firms that do have high standards. In one case, a development finance company associated with the World Bank Group assisted in the formation of a new accounting firm, with the understanding that if the firm would follow international accounting standards, the finance company would, in turn, underwrite the accounting firm's business until its operations were profitably established. The firm was an almost immediate success and is helping to establish a new norm for accounting practices in the country concerned.

Often the laws and legal practices of a country may be archaic when viewed in the light of modern business practice. Typical of this are security arrangements on loans and complications in matters of trusteeship. Legal traditions and customs may be difficult to modify, particularly if a significant amount of legislation is involved and the legislature is not business-oriented. By virtue of its operations, a development finance company will be aware of the areas in which financial operations are needlessly restricted by legislation and legal practices and it will be in a position, along with other interested parties, to suggest appropriate changes. Often development finance companies have good access to the legal experience and practices of other countries, and this can add to the effectiveness of their recommendations.

Developing a Trading Mechanism

The facilities available for trading of securities vary from the fairly adequate to nil. In most low income countries, there is some mechanism whereby the holders of various types of financial paper can liquidate their holdings. In some, bearer shares that require no registration of transfer are permitted, and there is considerable trading in these securities, although it may be neither efficient nor without substantial risk of fraud. In other countries, there may be small quantities of registered shares held by investors but no formal market, and thus all transfers are effected individually between buyer and seller. In still other countries, trading in securities may be limited to government securities at a price pegged by the government (normally by having the Central Bank buy and sell at par); in such cases, there is an exchange mechanism, although it cannot be considered a real trading mechanism since the price is fixed. In a few countries, security ownership may not exist at all, and there are consequently no procedures for exchanging either public or private securities.

Where no exchange exists or where the trading procedures are very rudimentary, a development finance company may play a role, often in cooperation with other institutions, in developing a trading mechanism. Some of these companies have been responsible for drafting legislation, establishing the regulations pertaining to an exchange mechanism, and establishing a share registration system. In such situations, the development finance company may even become a dealer and broker on the exchange and assist in its direction and management. Such activities are certainly of a developmental nature and any financial returns from these efforts will be indirect and will probably come only in the long run.

In a very small market, a useful first step may be merely the creation of some type of clearing house where individuals wishing to buy or sell can register their intent and the price at which they wish to do business; here could be kept records of transactions and the prices at which they were consummated. As trading increases, it may be necessary to establish a more formal exchange, with a daily or weekly call-over of listed securities; this would involve the legal establishment of the exchange, regulations for listing, and requirements as to who may act as brokers.

There are countries with established stock exchanges that list and trade only a few securities. Under these conditions existing mechanisms may not have gained public confidence, whether or not there has been improper supervision or speculative or fraudulent practices. Here the role of a development finance company might be the promotion of changes or reforms aimed at increasing the effectiveness of the exchange and at securing the confidence of the investing public in the exchange itself and in investment in securities in general. In countries where the mechanism for trading securities is moribund or discredited, remedies will be a prerequisite to broadening the capital market. However, it should be clear that what is required is not, necessarily, the existence of a formal stock exchange. This may or may not be needed, depending on circumstances. The basis for the development of securities ownership is mutual trust and confidence among those involved. If this element is missing or if it is called into question by fraudulent trading practices, the development of the capital market will be severely circumscribed, whatever the institutional facilities.

Expanding the Number of Securities Available

A development finance company may play an important role in another way, by increasing the number of private securities available in the local capital market, thereby diversifying investment alternatives.

Where industry is controlled by relatively small groups of local citizens, thus creating an unhealthy concentration of industrial wealth, an objective of the development finance company may be to get local firms to open their ownership to the public. In Pakistan, the Pakistan Industrial Credit and Investment Corporation considered requiring tightly held local firms to go public before lending to them. In a situation where capital is scarce, this could be an effective way of increasing the number of securities available. But it would of course lead to much opposition. The Pakistan Government subsequently put into effect a variant of this idea, and it is now required that 60 per cent of all capital *increases* of existing firms, or capitalizations of new firms, be offered to the public.

In countries where industrial development is in a stage in which foreign investment plays the predominant role in industrial development, the finance company may be in a position to encourage some of the existing or new foreign firms to offer some of their shares to the public and, if there is a stock exchange, to list such shares on the exchange. Although many foreign investors prefer to hold 100 per cent of the shares of the companies they have established, it is in the interest of both the country and the foreign investor that industry be closely identified with the local economy. Sometimes it will be not the capital it can thereby mobilize that will lead a foreign-held firm to offer its shares locally, but rather the psychological effect and the resulting improved "image." In Nigeria, for example, Icon Securities, a wholly owned subsidiary of the Nigerian Industrial Development Bank, has been quite effective in getting foreign firms to offer shares for sale to the public and to list their shares on the Lagos Stock Exchange.

A development finance company's ability to press for public issues will depend on its bargaining power vis-à-vis industrialists. It may be, for example, an important source of debt funds for these companies, and thus be in a position to make loans conditional on the issuance of shares to the public or to itself, with the understanding that it will later sell its portion of the shares to the public. If the development finance company's clients have confidence in its intentions, they may be more willing to make at least a gesture to outside participation in their firms by selling their shares to the development finance company. In some situations, the development finance company will have to exercise care when it "rolls over" its portfolio, in order that the ownership of a company not be altered in such a way as to create instability. More often, unless it holds a considerable proportion of the total share capital in a single firm, the development finance company should, after holding the investment for a time, aim at selling it to the public. In some countries, the current owners may be anxious to buy back the shares held by the development finance company, and here a decision must be made by management as to which is more important, the owners' retention of 100 per cent control or a wider distribution of shares.

Occasionally a development finance company may not be able to find industrial concerns it considers suitable for minority investors. This might be the case, for example, if the standards of business practices are low and the management of existing firms cannot be counted upon to operate in a responsible fashion with respect to minority shareholders. This is an extreme situation, but it does occur. When it does, there may be some justification for the development finance company to promote new companies and handpick major groups of shareholders in such a way as to give confidence that the management will deal forthrightly and honestly with all shareholders. The shares of such companies could be offered to the public with some confidence, either at the outset or at a later date, when the companies are well established. The Industrial Mining and Development Bank of Iran (IMDBI) has in fact done this in an environment where publicly held companies were previously unknown, by introducing new investors, such as financial institutions, and the new professional class, to the industrial sector. IMDBI thus led the way to the formation of industrial concerns in which ownership and management were separate. The trouble is that it will be difficult and costly for the development finance company to put together such projects; and the process may also result in a prolonged tie-up of its funds and more managerial responsibilities than it would normally wish to assume.

An inexperienced investing public will need to rely on the recommendations and examples of a development finance company. If that company can project itself in the eyes of the public as a competent and trustworthy institution, the fact that it is participating in an enterprise may be sufficient recommendation to private investors. Consequently, particularly at the early stages in the development of a capital market, it is very important that a development finance company be careful in the choice of the share issues it will support, in order to build confidence in its judgments. Some poor choices, early in its career, can do lasting damage to a development finance company's capacity to make an impact on the capital market.

Widening the Market for Securities

A development finance company can have a direct role in expanding the ownership of securities in two ways: by undertaking public issue work, and by underwriting sales of securities. In countries where the number of securities brokers and issuing houses is inadequate, a development finance company may find that it is in a position to take the lead in putting new securities before the public. At first, because of limitations of financial resources and the primitive condition of the capital market, it may not be able to underwrite industrial securities. Nevertheless, the company can make a start by offering to market industrial securities on a best efforts basis. This will involve it in the legal groundwork necessary to set up a public issue, the preparation of a prospectus, and the advertising and marketing of the shares. Occasionally the development finance company will have to operate entirely on its own, whereas in other cases, it may be able to join forces with other financial institutions in undertaking public issues. For example, the underwriting experiences of the Private Development Corporation of the Philippines, in a country where trading mechanisms and some limited stock brokerage exist, led PDCP to establish a unit within the Corporation whose major purpose was to work with financial institutions having good penetration throughout the country, such as insurance companies, using their offices and staffs as sales vehicles for new share offerings.

Public Issuance. Unlike the direct investment activities that development finance companies undertake, public issue work is primarily a marketing function. Consequently, it requires specialized skills different from those of the development finance company's regular staff. For this reason it may be advisable to establish a separate group within the company, or even a subsidiary company, to specialize in the marketing of securities.

An effective sales machine is a prerequisite to successful public issues and the problem is how to establish it. In the early stages of security ownership, the volume of sales and the brokerage income are likely to be marginal, so that the sales effort by banks and insurance companies will be motivated more by a spirit of public service than by the expectation of profit. This is particularly true if these institutions view the securities as eating into their own sources of funds from the public.

It is important that the sales effort be of high standard. When only a few people or institutions are involved, practices can be controlled by the self-discipline of the group, but as the system expands, it will be necessary to institute training and licensing procedures for dealers in securities and restrictions on who may sell them, as well as to regulate commissions. Here again the development finance company may take part in training and in designing controls to ensure the soundness of the issuing and dealing system.

Underwriting. Another step in broadening the market for securities is underwriting. In a relatively narrow capital market, this can involve considerable risk; for it will often be the newly established firms or new subsidiaries of existing firms that will seek to raise capital by way of public issues, and it will be the marginal share or debenture issues that will seek underwriting. Because of this narrowness, the underwriting skills necessary for success in low income countries may be different from those needed in developed countries.

In a broad and competitive capital market, with large amounts of funds coming into the market daily, an underwriting that is not fully sold indicates to the underwriting firm that the issuing price was wrong. The underwriter in this situation will not hold on to the security but will readjust his price in order to market the issue: in these conditions the basic underwriting skill is proper pricing. In a very thin market, however, the unsold portion of an underwriting operation may not indicate an unreasonable price, but rather a market so narrow that it cannot absorb the entire issue at a reasonable price.

In a narrow market the price necessary to sell a security may be unreasonably low, merely because the normal market for the security has absorbed all that it can. If this is the case, it may not be advisable to reduce the price in order to attract an entirely new and unexpected class of investor. The required skill, in such a situation, may not be in pricing but rather in estimating absolute levels of investable funds. A development finance company must therefore be prepared to operate as an investor as well as an underwriter. It may, on occasion, have to absorb into its own portfolio a large portion of a share or debenture issue. This possibility should impose a prudent caution on its underwriting decisions.

As the market for securities develops in volume, however, an underwriter may make pricing mistakes. By taking up the unsold balance for its own portfolio, the underwriter may be covering its error, and thereby penalizing its own shareholders. Its shareholders' interests should perhaps be the criterion for the development finance company's decision with respect to an unsold portion of an underwriting commitment. Are its shareholders best served by selling the issue at a reduced price or by holding on to it and selling it later at a better price?

Because of the risks of underwriting in thin markets, many development finance companies may have to do the bulk of their public issue work on a best efforts basis. It may be possible for them to arrange subunderwriting for an issue in advance of their own commitment; in this way, although they will have underwritten the issue, buyers will have been assured beforehand.

The brokerage and underwriting fees in the countries in which the development finance companies associated with the World Bank Group operate range from 2 per cent to 4 per cent for underwriting and brokerage is about $1\frac{1}{2}$ per cent. Because of the risk involved, these fees may not be realistic, but they are often fixed by the government, and the development finance company, as well as other underwriters, can only press for what they feel are reasonable rates. Rates too low to compensate for the risks of these operations will inhibit the growth of a capital market, rather than stimulate it.

Unit Trusts. Occasionally development finance companies have helped to establish some type of unit trust or mutual fund. The advantage here lies in offering the investor a diversified portfolio and professional management, even though he may make only a small investment. Whether it makes sense to establish a unit trust will probably depend on the number of securities available in a market and the opportunities for spreading risk. Governments often support such funds as a way of encouraging savings and may even give the funds tax advantages, thereby providing an additional benefit. What is important is to ensure competent and trustworthy management of the fund, sound sales methods, and realistic charges. In most cases, legislation will be needed to establish proper controls. A decision will also have to be made as to whether these funds should be private, based on making a profit for their owners, or government-controlled. Control should be determined by selecting the type of organization whose management will be the most effective in maximizing the interests of the fund's investors. There are serious pitfalls in establishing a fund or trust which has poor management or is considered to be a tool of public policy, subject to political pressures; such intermediaries cannot, in the long run, prove helpful in broadening a capital market.

When the question of unit trusts or mutual funds arises, a development finance company will generally have an interest in seeing to the establishment of sound institutions and the legislation relating to them, but depending on the environment it may or may not want to become directly involved in their formation and operations.

Sales out of Portfolio

The pricing problem is especially important to a development finance company in revolving its own funds, if the company is to achieve its three objectives of promoting security ownership, profit-taking and generating funds for further equity operations. The most straightforward method is to offer individual securities in the market at going prices or, if there is no market price, at the best available estimate of a market price. Variations in this method of marketing include giving first rights for purchase to the development finance company's own shareholders or selling blocks of its equity portfolio, made up of a combination of shares, in package deals. The problem in any sales maneuver, if the sales are not clearly priced according to the market, is that the institution exposes itself to possible unfairness to some or all of its shareholders, or to the purchasers of the shares. If its shareholders are given an option to buy at a lower than market price, only those in a position to buy will benefit, unless the rights are salable at market prices. If an effort is made to sell a package of shares to third parties, then price determination is extremely important so that advantage is taken of neither the purchasers nor the shareholders of the development finance company. If, however, pricing is done as fairly as possible, package sales or sales to shareholders may be a useful way of stimulating public interest in purchasing portions of a development finance company's portfolio and in creating interest in its own shares.

Maintaining an Orderly Market

Another aspect of promoting a capital market is the stabilization or maintenance of a market for securities, in order to avoid widely fluctuating prices. Where security ownership is not common, building up the confidence of the investing public in the investment of its savings in industrial securities is a prerequisite to expanding the number of investors and the volume of funds coming to the market. If market prices are erratic and the investor runs a considerable risk of not being able to liquidate his investment in a reasonable amount of time and at a reasonable price, investment in securities will be difficult to encourage. In very thin markets, there is a possibility of sharp fluctuations in prices as a result of rapidly changing conditions of supply and demand. The difficulty is that attempts to maintain an orderly market border on price maintenance of security values and this is something about which development finance companies should be extremely careful.

The variable most important to the role of a development finance company in trading securities is the size of the market. In a market of significant size, it is impossible for an institution with moderate resources to estabilize or fix the price of a given security at a level other than that established by the market. It might be able to do so temporarily, very briefly, but even this may be difficult. If a development finance company tries to hold the price of a security above the price the market is prepared to pay, the company will penalize its own shareholders; for the individual shareholders could buy the security at a lower price than their company is paying. It is their funds that are being used to pay the premium.

If, however, the number of shares traded and the volume of trading are low, and the number of shares of a given company in the hands of the public is relatively small, a good case can be made for the development finance company to maintain a pool of funds from which it is willing to sell and for which it is willing to buy to temper wide price fluctuations. This involves an element of price stabilization because the company must make a decision as to the price it is willing to pay and the price at which it is willing to sell the securities it is stabilizing. These decisions involve a significant risk. However, such activity can be very important for small industrial shareholders who may want to sell their $50–$100 investments on short notice. For them, a buyer prepared to take their shares at a price reflecting a realistic assessment of the position and prospects of the company whose shares they hold is vital. There is, however, a clear line between maintaining a market and maintaining a price. A development finance company can usefully maintain a market. But it should not support a security at a price that is unjustified in terms of the performance and prospects of the company involved. To do so would be to build a false confidence in the market, for the value of a security cannot be guaranteed. When considering "stabilization," a finance company must make a basic decision between its own profitability (and the interests of its shareholders) and its responsibility to the public and to the development of the securities market.

There is another reason for a development finance company to deal in the market: In a small market, relatively few people can set the price. In fact, if a development finance company is the most important broker, or perhaps the only broker, it may find itself in a position where buyers and sellers look to it for advice about a reasonable price for a given security. This situation is quite different from that in a developed capital market, where the opinions of many brokers and individual investors determine the market. In a narrow capital market, a broker may be dealing with both the buyer and the seller without the benefit of substantial outside sales to help him determine a market price. This places a great responsibility on the broker, but until a capital market reaches a size at which it is financially feasible for a number of people or institutions to engage in brokerage, the problems arising from such a narrow market will have to be dealt with by the managements of development finance companies.

This problem is dealt with by ICON Securities, the previously mentioned subsidiary of the Nigerian Industrial Development Bank, by maintenance of a pool of securities that ICON can trade into or out of on its own account. This has proved to be helpful to the small investor in a very thin market. The company's manager feels that it has been possible to play this role without maintaining unreasonable prices.

In countries with fairly well developed securities markets, such as India and Pakistan, the development finance company may not play a broker's role and these problems may not be relevant. On the other hand, in countries where capital markets are in their infancy, a development finance company may be called upon to do things that, though not orthodox in a broader and more fully developed capital market, are useful and necessary in generating the growth of the market. The fact that investors in a country may entirely lack experience in stock investment may even be an argument for a development finance company to issue shares to the public with an agreement to repurchase all or part of the issue from private investors within a given time, at a stipulated price. Such an arrangement should be carefully considered and the development finance company should not assume undue risk, but it could be a useful device for getting "people's feet wet" in the market.

From the foregoing, it is clear that there are no general rules by which a development finance company can "stabilize" a market or establish an "orderly market." Before engaging in such activity, a development finance company must consider the interests of its shareholders and must avoid supporting something that is economically unsupportable.

The Extent of Equity and Underwriting Activity

The main financial policy question relating to a development finance company's equity operations concerns the level of equity and underwriting operations. At present, most such companies restrict their equity acquisitions to an amount equivalent to their paid-in share capital and retained earnings. Underwriting commitments in excess of this are accepted if, in the management's view, the company will not have to take up the remains of an issue, which would put its equity holdings over its total aggregate worth. Some development finance companies have not found this guideline restrictive, for they have found it difficult to engage in equity operations because of the nature of the economies in which they operate and the prevailing structure of business. But others have gone more heavily into this field and have found that an equity limit equivalent to net worth tends to restrain their equity investments and underwriting operations. Thus the question arises as to whether this limit should be expanded or reduced.

This is a question to which there is no single "right" answer. The limitation of equity investments to the development finance company's own net worth is based on the assumption that equity operations are risky and uncertain of liquidation in emergency, and that a development finance company should therefore not use borrowed funds to make equity investments. In so doing, it would be undertaking a repayment obligation which might prove difficult to fulfill if the company were unable to liquidate equity investments at reasonable prices when cash was required for debt amortization.

It could in principle be argued that in some countries the capital market is so broad and buoyant that a finance company might, from time to time, consider it not only sound but advantageous to go into equities at a level exceeding its own net worth. By the same token, there might be situations in which the market and the risks were of such a nature that a development finance company would want to limit equity participations to something less than its own net worth. Neither should necessarily be a once-and-for-all policy; for market conditions and the risk inherent in equity operations can vary with a changing economic climate. It is a question that needs to be related to the company's cash flow, and to the stage of development of the capital market of the country concerned. If the company were in a relatively tight cash position, there would be less reason for increasing equity participations that might involve tying up funds for a considerable length of time than for reducing equity participations, thereby freeing resources for more liquid operations. If the cash position were strong and the market for securities were broad enough to give such investments a fair degree of liquidity, a stronger case could be made for an aggregate equity portfolio exceeding a development finance company's own net worth.

IV. CONCLUSIONS

In summary, development finance companies are often expected to play an important role in the promotion of the widespread ownership of industrial securities. In many countries they are in a unique position in terms of their staff, experience and resources to play such a role. What role they actually take will be dependent on the environment in which they operate. For those countries where capital markets are almost nonexistent, broadening the capital market will be a long, hard process and the development finance company operating in such a situation, although perhaps best placed among institutions to stimulate investment, should not be expected to achieve miracles overnight. There are a great many factors involved in determining whether or not conditions are conducive to the development of widespread security ownership and many of these are beyond the immediate control of the development finance company and the other financial institutions it works with. Whatever the obstacles to an active security market may be, however, an effective development finance company will normally have some role to play in encouraging the widespread ownership of securities and can often undertake activities directed toward this goal to the benefit of both its shareholders and the economy as a whole. Some of the development finance companies associated with the World Bank Group are doing pioneer work in this area of activity.

3

RELATIONSHIP BETWEEN A DEVELOPMENT FINANCE COMPANY AND THE MANAGEMENT OF ENTERPRISES IT PROMOTES, SPONSORS, OR FINANCES

by E. T. Kuiper

INTRODUCTORY NOTE

When a development finance company promotes, sponsors or finances an enterprise, it risks its capital and reputation; and it often influences others, both individuals and institutions, to risk their capital as well. This is a grave responsibility, which requires continuing vigilance on the part of the finance company.

That responsibility calls, in the first place, for the careful selection of investment proposals. No factor in selection is more important than a judgment regarding management, and a decision that management is satisfactory—technically, commercially, administratively, and in terms of honesty. But satisfaction with management before the investment is made is not enough. Management remains a matter of continuing concern thereafter. This is important when a development finance company has given a loan to the enterprise; it is critical when the enterprise is a promotion of the company.

Dr. José Gutierrez Gomez, President of the Corporación Financiera Nacional of Colombia, who was chairman of the discussion, pointed out at least three aspects of this Agenda item. One concerned the financiera's problem of obtaining full and timely information on the affairs of his client; another in-

volved taking a seat on the board of directors of the client enterprise; a third was involvement in day-to-day decision making. On the first, there was no dissent on the fundamental importance of having at all times a current knowledge of the situation of a client enterprise and of establishing a close and constructive relationship with it. And on the third, there was a strong reluctance against participating in management. But on the taking of a board seat, opinions differed widely, from the completely negative through abstemiousness to a positive conviction that a board seat established a desirable relationship not otherwise possible.

Dr. Gutierrez Gomez felt that conventional end-use, supervision and board representation could be equally effective in establishing the right kind of relationship between a development finance company and the management of its client enterprise. A director could do much effective missionary work, but a great deal depended on luck in the selection of a director and on the habits and procedures of the board on which he sat. Many participants shared his concern about the difficulty of finding qualified outside directors and the risks of taking directors from inside—risks of overburdening management, creating conflicts of interest, and compromising the future business of the development finance company. These risks were magnified when a company took on managerial responsibilities. In general a tendency to abstain pervaded the discussion, despite recognition of the need to go the limit in cases of jeopardy and in some cases of promotion.

I. BASIC PERSPECTIVE

It is often said that, in the less developed countries, where most of the development finance companies connected with the World Bank Group operate, there is an appalling lack of managerial ability, and that this constitutes one of the principal difficulties in fostering industrial growth and creates a major risk for financiers of new industrial ventures. So general a statement as that needs qualification. In many of the countries that are now on the road to industrial development, there is no dearth of commercial know-how. What is even more important, from an organizational point of view, one finds in them a number of men who have a real talent for inspiring their associates. In Asian and African countries there are many families which have been in business for generations and have developed groups of people who work together in harmony under centralized, often more or less patriarchal leadership for a common purpose. In an organizational sense, this should be an invaluable asset, and one which is no longer so widely spread as it once was in Europe or the United States.

But the statement that there is a lack of managerial ability may still be justified. A community cannot depend for its industrial development exclusively on the few groups which have built up commercial organizations in the past. Moreover, these traditional businessmen sometimes find it difficult to adapt their views and methods to the administrative requirements of large-scale modern industrial ventures. New attitudes towards management are needed because as an enterprise grows, capital has to be attracted from outsiders and new techniques may call for the employment of foreign technicians and managers.

Nevertheless, the staff of a development finance company, which is often oriented to modern organizational patterns, should always value the qualities of commercial acumen and organizational know-how that are present in the communities they serve. It is obvious that good management is the key to the success of any enterprise. The development banker would do well to recognize that he should be careful when trying to impose his own ideas on his clients because there is more than one way to manage an industrial venture. The relationship between development finance companies and their clients involves a two-way traffic; even the best qualified banker has to learn a lot before he can start to teach or to guide. The managers of the development finance companies associated with the World Bank Group recognize that, even where they have the power to force their views on their client companies, it is the latter which should in practically all circumstances remain fully responsible. Only if, after very careful consideration, there remains a basic incompatability of views on important matters and the investment of the company is in jeopardy, ought the company use whatever powers it may have to replace management.

In this perspective, one can consider the three ways in which a development finance company maintains regular contact with its clients and gives advice to it under the following headings:

(1) obtaining information,
(2) representation on boards of directors, and
(3) taking responsibility for or participation in management.

An essential difference between ordinary commercial banking on the one hand and development financing on the other is that the latter is not primarily concerned with tangible security that can easily be realized, but takes a long-term view of a venture's financial prospects. The personal and financial standing of the people sponsoring an enterprise is also, of course, of considerable importance.

Before a financial deal, whether a loan, a participation, or an agreement to underwrite, is concluded, a project is carefully studied by the development finance company and forecasts are made in a joint exercise with the project's sponsors. This period of project preparation and financial negotiation usually presents suitable occasions to suggest improvements in many aspects of the venture, so that the development finance company may in effect play a crucial role in influencing its structure. It is at this stage that the banker and the client get to know each other better, and it is here that the relationship of mutual confidence should take shape. The foundation of confidences laid then, if it is well done, will assume a mutually beneficial relationship between a development finance company and the client after the transaction has been finalized and the banker's money is actually invested.

II. OBTAINING INFORMATION

It is a common experience that management and staff devote much more time and effort to project preparation and loan negotiations than to keeping themselves well informed concerning the activities of clients in whose businesses their institutions' money is at risk. Yet it is extremely important to keep in close touch with clients. Personal contacts on the technical and policy levels are needed, but no less important are more formal relationships, through regular audits and end-use inspections, i.e., frequent, periodic assessments of performance in construction of the project and in running the enterprise when construction is done. If this is to be done, provision must be made in the loan contract to give the development finance company the right to ask for information and to carry out inspections, imposing on the borrower the obligation to supply all information required. The discrepancies between projection and performance, and the problems that come to light from the reports and during the inspections form a useful subject for discussion between the financiers and the client, and lead to opportunities for consultation about measures for improvements. Usually, but not always, the client himself knows his own business best, but the development finance company may have a broader range of experience from which suggestions can be drawn to help a specific client.

Follow-up investigations are, generally, carried out by the staff of the development finance company, but it is often useful to enlist the services of independent consultants. It is usually a condition of a loan contract that the client must retain independent auditors satisfactory to the development bank and that the auditors should be chosen from a panel presented by them to their customers. Such audits should be made available as a matter of routine; they, with other detailed reports, create the foundation for a constructive relationship.

Every banker has much to learn from his clients; unless he is willing to learn more every day about the special intricacies of particular situations, he will soon find it impossible to maintain a relationship of confidence. It also should constantly be realized that the managers of these enterprises remain responsible for its operations; unless they can be convinced that a suggestion makes sense, it is useless to try to force it upon them. The aim of the development banker should be to create such an atmosphere of confidence that his opinion and advice are asked and his suggestions are accepted in the knowledge that they are based on experience and common interest.

III. REPRESENTATION ON BOARDS OF DIRECTORS

Development finance companies do not restrict themselves to loan operations. They often venture out into more entrepreneurial activities by participating in new or reorganized enterprises, by underwriting or by financing in one way or another a very substantial amount of the total cost of a venture. In these cases the matter of relationship with clients may take on new aspects. Information and inspection may not be sufficient. A seat on the board of directors may be called for.

Obtaining accurate and reliable information from a client and carrying out follow-up inspections are crucial. It is doubtful whether the position of a financial institution in this respect can be improved by taking a seat on the board of the enterprise. Experience shows that directors are often less well informed than are the bankers who take follow-up procedures seriously. Indeed, sometimes an institution tends to relax vigilance when it has a director on the board, and to rely mainly on board papers or on the views of the individual who happens to serve as its representative on the board.

Experience differs widely in this respect because no two boards operate in the same manner. For instance, some boards meet every week, and others once a year. Sometimes board meetings are cut-and-dried affairs; sometimes discussion in the board brings out facets of an operation that cannot be appreciated in another manner. What is important in this respect is the personal relations established between directors and managers and the candid opinions expressed during meetings which are usually not placed on record.

Another advantage of a directorship involves the timeliness of information and of possible intervention. Audits, reporting and follow-up inspections are retroactive, in the sense that they inform after the event. On the other hand, a board is normally informed of prospective decisions before they are taken; a development finance company represented on a board may often have a chance to put in a word at the most opportune moment, and then exercise an influence which follow-up, audits, and reports will not allow.

When a financial institution puts a director on the board of a client enterprise it obtains for itself certain powers which go beyond those reserved in a loan contract. At the same time it assumes a measure of responsibility that may, especially in the case of an enterprise whose shares are held by the public, constitute an onerous burden. Newly floated companies, especially, which a development finance company has promoted, sponsored, or underwritten and whose shares it has helped market, may ask the company to go on its board because this enhances its standing. Indeed going on the board may be a measure required for effective sponsorship, promotion, or underwriting. There is, however, understandable reluctance on the part of development finance companies to accept such nominations because they might in this manner be faced with a conflict of interest (for instance, on dividend policy) between that of the shareholding public and that of the financier. Some development finance companies have found that board representation has strengthened an otherwise tenuous relationship with a debtor company; others have felt it wiser to remain aloof so as to avoid being in a situation in which sides have to be taken with either of the factions one often finds fighting more or less openly in a board.

The situation appears in a different light when the finance company is itself an important shareholder and not simply a debtor. It is not only unusual, but in many countries it is illegal, for specific shareholders to procure for themselves privileges in the matter of information or otherwise; therefore a directorship may be the only way for the institution to keep itself informed and to try to influence management when that seems desirable.

Sometimes a development finance company is asked to go on the board of an enterprise where foreign and indigenous entrepreneurs each own a certain portion of the stock. This may not be an enviable position in every respect, but the finance company may have to take on the responsibilities of a "go-between" in order to help bring, and hold, together varying interests, especially if it took the initiative in bringing those interests together.

Clearly there are many pros and cons on the issue of putting representatives on boards of client enterprises. The finance companies associated with the World Bank Group have widely differing views on the subject. In general, they seemed agreed that they should be represented on boards when they owned an amount of stock large enough to justify such representation. But there was no concession on whether to take a seat on the board of a company to which a loan had been given. Some felt a finance company should never go on the board of a debtor company; other institutions invariably take the right to nominate a director, but exercise it sparingly. None seemed keen to put nominees on boards of debtor companies because this usually involved the financial institutions in responsibilities and conflicts of interest without giving it extra powers; but it was generally agreed that there is sometimes no suitable alternative to protect the interest of the institution, of the public, or of a particular enterprise.

When it is decided to put a representative on the board, an appropriate person must be chosen. Who? Some development finance companies prefer to have members of their own staff on clients' boards, because they feel this strengthens the relationship. Others prefer qualified outsiders, because they would not so directly involve the development finance companies in responsibilities or differences of opinion. The latter group generally admit, however, that it is difficult to find qualified people who could and would take time to interest themselves sufficiently in the affairs of the client companies. One company expressed the opinion that qualified people should be found prepared to specialize in the responsibilities of industrial directorship and should develop such specialization as a professional career.

IV. PARTICIPATION IN MANAGEMENT?

The General Case Against Involvement

Development finance companies are, and have good reason to be, reluctant to take seats on boards of directors. It is not surprising that, as a rule, development banks refuse to be involved in management. There is sometimes only a thin line between a board seat and participation in management. The line is nevertheless there.

First, there is the human angle. A good development banker should have some entrepreneurial and managerial qualities, but he is usually stronger on the financial, technical and administrative sides. More important still is the institutional aspect. A development finance company is set up to serve many clients in each of many fields of industrial activity, and it should not identify itself with the interest of one particular enterprise in one particular field; by doing so it risks compromising its position vis-à-vis other businesses in the same industry. Finally, there is the financial principle that a development bank should place its investments with prudence and with proper diversification. Involvement of a development finance company in the management of a company would mean that two functions are merging into one; the function of the entrepreneur who should go ahead, take risks, expand, and the function of the financier who should ask questions, restrain, and urge caution.

Notwithstanding these sound arguments against involvement of a development finance company in managerial responsibilities, there are exceptional cases where such responsibilities should be undertaken. Three instances may be cited which are symptomatic of the cases when deviation from an admirably sound principle is necessary.

The Exceptions

As noted in the discussion of promotion, in some countries clients with constructive ideas and funds to back them are conspicuously absent, yet the development finance company feels there are really promising possibilities. The company then has to take the responsibility for promoting; for if it does not do this, nobody else will. In such a situation, there is often no alternative to involvement in management if the promotion is to be successful. This is a risky business but sometimes an unavoidable one; it is a type of "priming" which contributes to the industrial development of the country.

One finds in some countries enterprises that are now widely held which are still managed by men who, years earlier, were put into managerial posts by the development banks on whose staffs they worked. In another country, a development finance company has been asked to administer a portfolio of government participations in industry. It may find that some of these enterprises need reorganization and that it is not in all cases possible to find qualified outside managers. In such instances the finance company may delegate one or more of its staff to form a management team, which is accountable to the company, and which will, hopefully, be replaced one day.

Still another kind of case involves jeopardy. In the case of an investment gone sour, the taking over of management may offer the only alternative to outright loss.

Thus, the development finance companies which have entered, directly or indirectly, into the management of the client enterprise have never done so lightly, and have done so in the conviction that there was no acceptable alternative and that the situation would be temporary.

V. CONCLUSIONS

Good management is of crucial importance for the success of new enterprises, and one of the most important tasks for a development finance company is to encourage good management and to establish close and constructive contacts with its clients. The possession of reliable and up-to-date information is a prerequisite in this respect.

Responsibility for management should remain where it belongs—with the owners of the enterprise—and for this reason development finance companies are often reluctant to accept directorships and always reluctant to manage the industrial enterprise they finance. There may be cases, however, when a development bank has to go on a board, primarily when a share participation justifies such action, but also when it is felt that reliable information cannot be obtained otherwise or when the bank's interests need extra surveillance. Managerial responsibilities are also on rare occasions accepted but only when doing so is justified as a temporary measure for which there is no reasonable alternative.

4

FINANCIAL POLICY PROBLEMS
OF DEVELOPMENT FINANCE COMPANIES

by Douglas Gustafson

INTRODUCTORY NOTE

The Agenda of the Conference called for a discussion of the financial policy of development finance companies. Included were such diverse matters as the level of debt a development finance company can prudently incur, policy towards the establishment of reserves to protect the company against specific expected losses, how much of profits should be paid out and how much retained, the effect of taxation on reserves policy and dividend payments, and interest rate policy. Thus "financial policy" was not "a subject," but a package of subjects.

It was also a complex and important package of subjects, especially for institutions which were approaching maturity —for they were fundamental to decisions on how the growth of development finance companies was to be financed. They were also subjects on which there could be conflicts of interest among interested parties—certainly between shareholders and creditors; and perhaps also governments, if governments were providing important financial resources or incentives.

The chairman of the discussion of financial policy was Mr. H. T. Parekh, General Manager of the Industrial Credit and Investment Corporation of India. The largest part of the discussion concerned the level of debt. Mr. Parekh noted that, if a development finance company is to make satisfactory profits, its ratio of debt to equity must be weighted in favor of its shareholders. As a lender, he insisted that his borrowers maintain a 1:1 ratio, but as a borrower he preferred to have no limit. Such a stand was not defensible; there had to be some check. On the other hand, development finance companies could not afford to close their doors; business had to be increased. If so, they needed resources. Local currency funds had been relatively easy to raise, for governments were not bothered about debt-equity ratios. But the World Bank and other conventional lenders did ask questions which, while relevant, were sometimes disagreeable. In the past, the World Bank had been most helpful by relaxing the limitation, when the situation justified a relaxation. Still, financial institutions had to recognize that there were limits to the debt they could incur, even from the point of view of their own prudence. Mr. Parekh pointed out that part of the difficulty lay in the fact that raising equity capital was the most expensive form of financing and that it was difficult to go to the market for new capital until additional capital could be serviced without reduction of reserves.

On another aspect of financial policy, Mr. Parekh called attention to the difficulty of establishing a "right" balance between retention of earnings and payment of dividends. The former encouraged creditors, the latter encouraged investors. The former was needed for nationally financed growth; the latter for external financing. In either case the attitude of the shareholder was crucial: how and at what price did he want to finance the growth of the development finance company? Mr. Parekh felt that a 50-50 distribution was a reasonable rule of thumb. Regarding interest spreads, the general feeling was that a spread of $2\frac{1}{2}$ per cent to 3 per cent was reasonable. As to whether the interest charged should be above or below the prevailing market rates, Mr. Parekh thought a lower interest might attract bad projects while a higher rate might adversely affect a development finance company's public image. On the question of taxation, Mr. Parekh considered it politically inexpedient to ask for total tax exemption, although a case could be made that, since a development finance company's operations involve large risks, profits put to reserve should not be taxed to the same extent as distributed profits. There is another tax concession that in many cases would be very beneficial in the raising of new resources. This would be tax exemption for development finance company bond issues. Clearly, the crucial question a development finance company would face over the years was that of raising resources, both loan and equity, in order to continue to expand operations. Although financial assistance could be expected for some time from governmental sources and international institutions, it would become necessary for a development finance company to go the market at some stage, and it was thus essential to gear financial policies to facilitate this objective.

The discussions and Mr. Parekh's summing up made it clear that there were no easy or universal answers to the questions that had been raised.

I. MAIN ELEMENTS OF THE PROBLEM

Doing Business in Terra Incognita

The development finance companies associated with the World Bank Group are in many respects crossing uncharted territory. They are unique in most of the countries where they operate, in the kind of financing they do, in their appraisal and follow-up efforts, and in their methods of financing their operations. Although charged with a developmental function, they are also responsible for earning a return satisfactory to their shareholders. To achieve these goals, it has been necessary to develop new types of financial structures and policies. For many of these development finance companies, previous comparable experience, which could serve as a sound guideline for their operations, is not available in their countries; and even the older ones among them have an experience of only about ten years or so, which, relatively speaking, is a very short history. Yet within this time some of these institutions have accumulated large resources and occupy an important position in the fabric of industrial and financial institutions in their countries. Because of their unique features and the absence of institutional history, they have had to develop new financial policies determined, in many cases, by environment and circumstances, and in others, by intuition. This underlies the difficulty of trying to use an analytical approach in defining financial policy, particularly for a new type of company.

Unfortunately, some of the knottiest problems of financial policy are fundamental to the sound growth of a development finance company. How much debt should a development finance company incur relative to the shareholders' equity? On what terms should this debt be acquired, and how do these terms affect the overall acceptable level of debt? What interest spreads are required? How should losses and bad debt allowances be handled? What is the appropriate dividend and reserve policy in a given environment? These are basic questions of financial policy which must concern the shareholders, management, and creditors of a private development finance company, and they are the subjects considered here. It is an important task of those associated with development finance companies to sharpen the decision-making process used in answering these questions.

Diversity of Development Bank Capital Structure

Although there is similarity among the development finance institutions associated with the World Bank Group, each operates in its distinctive environment and has its unique characteristics. Generalization is always difficult and sometimes impossible. For instance, capital structures differ widely. Some companies have been launched with what might be called a World Bank "model" capital structure consisting of 100 units of share capital, a thirty-year interest-free loan of 150 units, subordinate to share capital, and an initial borrowing power of three times the sum of these, or 750 units. This borrowing power allows a maximum of nine units of debt capital for every unit of shareholders' equity. A variation of this is a company that has a share capital of 100 units, a thirty-year low-interest loan of 300 units, subordinate to other debt but ranking ahead of paid-in share capital, and an initial borrowing power of three times the sum of these, or 1,200 units; this structure allows a maximum of fifteen units of debt to be mobilized for each unit of shareholders' equity. Still other companies do not have subordinated loans but have been entrusted with the management of funds belonging to their governments, which they have invested in industry without risk and with a fixed income. Finally, some development finance companies associated with the World Bank Group have no subordinated loans or agency funds, and operate under government- or creditor-imposed borrowing limits ranging from 3 to 6.6 times their own net worth.

Diversity of Goals of Financial Policy

Although the capital structures of the score of companies associated with the World Bank Group are varied, the objectives of their financial policies are more uniform. But each company must serve several goals.

In any private concern, the primary responsibility of the management is to the company's shareholders. Financial policies of development banks, like all their policies, should be directed, in the first instance, toward earning a reasonable return for the shareholders and, second, toward the related goal of maintaining an organization capable of expanding its resources with a minimum of special concessions. The ability to expand resources is indicated by the ability of the company to raise additional equity capital as well as to obtain loan capital on suitable terms.

However, these basic objectives are somewhat clouded by the fact that private development finance companies are hybrid institutions, which, although distinctively private, are also involved in activities that are not reflected in their financial statements. These less easily measured activities motivate both governments and private shareholders to provide funds on a broader basis than merely financial return. Governments often feel that the overall economic impact of a development finance company warrants the provision of funds on nonmarket terms, if this is necessary to bring the company into existence and to sustain its activity. Occasionally shareholders realize benefits corollary to the financial return on their investment, and they purchase shares in this knowledge. These factors are almost always of great importance during the formative stage of a development finance company; and there may, in fact, be companies for which such concessions are necessarily and justifiably a continuous feature of their operations.

Nevertheless the managements of such companies feel that a company operating in the private sector must have as a goal the minimization of special concessions. Capital provided on concessional terms is more likely to result in undesirable restrictions on a management's freedom than funds that are obtained competitively in the market.

In order to be able to expand resources, a development finance company must maintain financial policies that will both attract private investors so that new share capital will be forthcoming when needed and leave creditors satisfied in order that loan capital will continue to be available. Obviously conditions vary greatly from country to country and subjective responses influence the decisions of investors and creditors, so that it is not possible to take a given company and formulate, on the basis of a completely rational analysis, a precise financial policy.

II. DEBT-EQUITY RELATIONSHIPS

Perhaps the most fundamental questions of financial policy for a development finance company concern the appropriate level of debt, relative to equity, and what the terms of that debt should be. The complexity of this problem has often led to simplifications and rules of thumb that are based primarily on what has been done before rather than on an analysis of what is appropriate for a given company at a given time.

The Aims of Shareholders

In practice, there are two distinct approaches to the determination of the relationship between debt and equity.

Generally, shareholders are interested in maximizing the financial return on their investment; this viewpoint, in the case of a development finance company, leads to maximizing the number of units of "outside" capital (debt or managed funds) for every unit of equity whether in the form of paid-in share capital or of retained earnings. If given the choice, shareholders will always prefer to increase debt relative to equity (i.e., increase leverage) as long as they feel that the marginal net spread on new debt resources, after all charges, including losses, is positive. Take, for example, a company which earns a gross spread of 2½ per cent on borrowed funds, whose administrative expenses and taxes at the margin take 1½ per cent, and whose expected annual losses on the company's portfolio are steady at ½ per cent. The net spread on these funds would be ½ per cent; and shareholders would, in principle, like to expand debt relative to equity infinitely. If, for any number of reasons, increased debt were to produce no net margin or a negative one, shareholders would not, of course, want to incur the new debt.

The Aims of Creditors

Creditors, on the other hand, are concerned with risk. Therefore, they wish to maintain an expectation of repayment of their funds commensurate with the interest rates they charge.

It is clear that the final decision as to what is appropriate involves a balance between the views of the shareholder and those of the creditor. However, because the evaluation of risk is such a difficult task, debt-versus-equity decisions are largely a matter of judgment based on what those involved are accustomed to. An analytical formulation of what is a "right" debt-equity policy is difficult, if not impossible.

A Single Useful but Inadequate Solution

The management of a development finance company, representing, as it should, the shareholders, may often use the following approach in determining a reasonable debt-equity policy. First, it establishes a minimum acceptable return on equity; then it imposes on this the spread earned on its resources. With these two conditions stipulated, the management then determines the leverage necessary to achieve the desired result. This simple arithmetical way of arriving at a decision is helpful in that it indicates what may be necessary in a given situation to maintain a profitable operation.

The fact, however, that a given relationship of debt to equity is necessary, given certain spreads, to make a development finance company reasonably profitable does not in any way indicate whether that debt-equity relationship is appropriate from a risk standpoint and will therefore be acceptable to creditors.[1] The major concern of creditors is the measurement of their risk; this involves an analysis of their client's risk under what might be considered normal operating conditions and possible deviations from the normal. Such measurements probably constitute the most difficult of all financial problems.

III. ANALYSIS OF THE DEBT-EQUITY PROBLEM WITH THE WORLD BANK MODEL

The World Bank "model" capital structure for a development finance company, referred to above, provides a useful base for examining the problem. There was no experience by

[1] On the other hand, if a company operating under an established debt-equity relationship is earning returns that the market judges attractive, it is not reasonable to expect that creditors will be willing to increase their risk by increasing their exposure in the company, relative to shareholders' equity; they will want to be compensated in some way for the additional risk they thereby assume.

which to judge the proper relationship among shareholders' equity, subordinated loans, and conventional loans for this new type of company. The initial ratios were determined, not by analytical findings as to what was reasonable in a particular economy for a particular company doing a particular kind of business, but rather by a feeling that the "model" capital structure was reasonable. The managements of many of these companies have not had to question the appropriateness of this initial debt-equity relationship; for the younger companies, the problem of the relative amounts of outside capital to shareholders' capital is not important, since it takes several years before a company's initial borrowing capacity is fully utilized. Experience to date with this capital structure has not been unfavorable. A number of companies operating with it have been reasonably profitable, and their creditors have incurred no losses.

Subordinated Loans

Role of Subordinated Loans from the Shareholder's Viewpoint. Except in Colombia, Greece, Spain, and Venezuela, subordinated loans or managed funds have been put at the disposal of development finance companies associated with the World Bank Group by local governments, or by the United States government at the request of local governments. This was done largely at the urging of the World Bank, which considered such funds appropriate for the formation of these private companies. The funds provide an initial earning base at little or no cost to the shareholders, as well as a base for considerable leverage. Although it is common among these companies to refer to their capital structures as having a debt-equity ratio of 3:1, this is not correct, because the potential ratio of real debt to equity, which reflects the actual leverage on shareholders' equity, is on the order of 9:1.

Another important aspect of some subordinated loans, from the shareholders' point of view, is that they usually give the shareholders additional protection; if the company goes into liquidation, the share capital ranks either ahead of, or pari passu with, the subordinated funds. In other cases, these funds rank ahead of share capital and are subordinated only to foreign debt. The relative ranking of subordinated funds, reserves and paid-in share capital is not material to the risk position of creditors who have supplied senior debt, because their exposure is determined by the total amount of funds which are junior to their loans.

Role of Subordinated Loans from the Lender's Viewpoint. The providers of subordinated funds have often made them available without a detailed consideration of their exposure and risk position in the borrowing company. Such loans have been made generally because the World Bank considers them a reasonable and necessary component of a development finance company's capital structure. As a practical matter, governments supplying funds to private development finance companies have often given the World Bank Group the responsibility for overseeing a "proper" capital structure. They have been prepared to take the World Bank's advice even though it involves them, as subordinate lenders, in the greatest financial risk among all those who provide capital to the proposed company. In some cases, the only protection that a subordinated creditor has, apart from confidence in the management of the company and confidence in the World Bank's concern for the company's continuing stability, is a contractual provision that the company set aside a certain part of earnings in reserves. Such a provision gives some backstopping to a loan subordinated to paid-in share capital, for the subordinated loan usually ranks ahead of retained earnings in liquidation. On occasion, however, subordinated creditors have not explicitly concerned themselves with reserve build-up and have left the whole question of proper debt-equity relationships to the World Bank Group.

Theoretically, creditors making different classes of loan funds available to a development finance company should select a different debt-equity ratio for each type of debt. This does not, however, happen in practice; what has happened is that the World Bank has, on its own, selected the ratios of non-subordinated debt to shareholders' equity plus subordinated loans for most of the companies associated with it.[2]

Problems of Maturity. Although relatively young development finance companies are not greatly concerned with debt-equity decisions, as they mature and press against their original borrowing limits and as they face the prospect of having to repay subordinated loan funds originally included as part of

---

[2] In some cases, however, not all of the subordinated funds available to the company have been included in its borrowing base. Such a situation usually reflects, when it occurs, the non-analytical reliance on intuition referred to earlier.

their borrowing base, the concern for establishing an appropriate capital structure becomes of major importance. In most cases there are pressures to redefine debt limitations so that the companies may take on additional debt. Illustrative of these pressures is the case of a company with a debt limitation of three times a borrowing base made up of net worth plus a subordinated loan, and an earnings spread, after financial charges and administrative expenses, of 2 per cent on capital employed. This company might grow as follows:

		Year A	Year B	Year C	Year D
(a)	Paid-in share capital	100	100	125	150
(b)	Retained earnings	....	50	75	150
(c)	Net worth	100	150	200	300
(d)	Subordinated debt included in borrowing base	150	150	75	....
(e)	Borrowing base	250	300	275	300
(f)	Other debt (3 × e)	750	900	825	900
(g)	Total capital	1,000	1,200	1,100	1,200
(h)	Earnings (2% of total capital)	20	24	22	24
(i)	Return on net worth	20%	16%	11%	8%
(j)	Ratio of total debt to net worth (d + f/c)	9:1	7:1	4.5:1	3:1

The company's problems, as it matures, can be summarized as follows:

(1) Real leverage, i.e., the ratio of outside funds to shareholders' funds, declines between year A and year B as reserves increase, although all the subordinated funds remain intact.

(2) This loss of leverage is accelerated when the subordinated debt is lost through repayment.

(3) The result is a decline in the return on shareholders' equity.

(4) As long as the earnings increment on new borrowed funds is positive, raising additional debt will be cheaper, from the existing shareholders' point of view, than increasing the paid-in share capital.

(5) Furthermore, although this is not illustrated in the example, it is likely that low-interest funds become a smaller proportion of the total resources of a development finance company as it matures. Thus the average cost of its capital will increase, and the average earnings spread on resources employed will drop.

Whether there is an overall decline in the margin will depend on the movement of administrative expenses, as well as bad debt losses, relative to the resources employed.

(6) In addition to these normal forces, there is always the possibility that market conditions and the company's operations are such that it may not be possible to go to the market to sell new ordinary shares at a price that existing shareholders would consider reasonable.

It is clear that as this company nears its initial borrowing capacity and the time when it must begin to repay its subordinated loans, it faces an entirely new set of problems concerning the continuity of its earnings potential and the expansion of its resources. There is thus a strong motivation, from the shareholders' point of view, to have the borrowing limit relaxed in order to maintain actual leverage. Several of the development finance companies associated with the World Bank Group are in this situation, or approaching it.

The Case Where Subordinated Funds Predominate. Another interesting situation occurs when a company continues to receive local currency loans that are subordinated to foreign debt or when other unusual circumstances exist in which subordinate funds are very large, relative to the company's own net worth. For example, the original capital structure of the Industrial Credit and Investment Corporation of India (ICICI) consisted of Rs50 million in paid-in share capital and Rs75 million in a long-term government loan subordinate to share capital and other debt. ICICI's agreement with the World Bank limited the company's borrowing to three times the sum of these funds, allowing an effective leverage of 9:1. By the end of 1965, ICICI's net worth had increased to Rs94 million and, in addition to the original Rs75 million of subordinated debt, ICICI had obtained from the Government of India additional loans of Rs220 million. Although not subordinated to share capital, these loans were subordinated to foreign debt. If the Rs220 million were included in the borrowing base along with the original government loan of Rs75 million, the total level of senior debt that this borrowing base allows would have been Rs1,556 million and the ratio of outside funds (all debt) to shareholders' funds at this limit would be on the order of 20:1. Even at this level of borrowing, the exposure of foreign creditors in ICICI would still be on the basis of a ratio of 4:1; from the viewpoint of their risk, this would not be unreasonable. But would a ratio of debt to equity of 20:1 be a healthy situation for ICICI?

The case of the Industrial Development Bank of Turkey (TSKB) is similar. At no risk to itself, this company had been managing TL382 million in agency funds for the government. The company's own net worth in 1966 amounted to approximately TL76 million and it had been borrowing, principally foreign currency funds, on the basis of a limit of four times its net worth. In 1966 the managed funds were turned over to TSKB in the form of a long-term loan, subordinated both to other debt and to share capital. If this subordinated loan is included in TSKB's borrowing base on the 4:1 ratio, the company would be able to borrow funds, both subordinate and conventional debt, up to a total amount of almost twenty-eight times its net worth. Here again, the infusion of additional subordinated loan capital and the potentially high total ratio of debt to equity have not increased the risk to conventional creditors in case of default; it is clearly the junior creditor (i.e., the government) who assumes the additional risk.

The Establishment of "Proper" Ratios

The Problem. The World Bank's attitude toward debt-equity relationships is broader than that of a normal creditor. The Group, as promoter, financial adviser, creditor, and shareholder of private development finance companies, has a much wider responsibility, and some governments rely on it to exercise this responsibility. The Bank's objective is twofold: that the company be solvent, profitable, and eventually self-sustaining, and that the risk taken by creditors, including subordinated creditors, be at an acceptable level. Its first objective coincides with that of the company's management and shareholders. As for the second, the World Bank is, in effect, asked to decide the overall level and the terms of debt that are acceptable in order to avoid an excessive risk of insolvency. What are the risks? What level of risk are the creditors and shareholders willing to accept?

Any answer to these questions will be riddled with judgments. For an industrial concern, the rational approach to debt decisions is to evaluate the behavior of each major determinant of the company's cash flow (taking into account its realizable assets) in a recessionary period, on the basis of the past experience of the company and of similar companies in the same industry during a business downturn. It is extremely difficult to forecast the severity and length of a recession and its impact on a company's sales and costs. This must nevertheless be done; critical judgment must be exercised in trying to quantify these forecasts. Shareholders and creditors alike must endeavor to make systematic analyses of cash flows in order to rationalize the decision-making process a step beyond the application of hunches and rules of thumb.

Similarly, in endeavoring to establish a reasonable debt-equity relationship for a development finance company, an attempt should be made to evaluate the company's operations under normal operating conditions and to forecast cash flows under adverse circumstances, assuming different levels of debt and equity and different terms for the various levels of debt. Conceptually, the approach is basically the same for a finance company as for an industrial concern. In undertaking this analysis, however, two important differences should be noted.

Firstly, for an industrial concern, the important variables are sales and costs. For a development finance company, normal expenses can be forecast with relative accuracy and the major variable determinant of the cash flow will be the estimated net defaults in a recessionary period (net defaults being gross defaults on interest and principal in a given period less cash recoveries by the realization of security during that period).

Secondly, if the development finance company is borrowing for periods longer than it is lending, the chances are that it can generate a large cash-flow surplus by making no new loans under normal operating circumstances. By stopping new operations, the excess of debt collection from its customers over debt repayments to its creditors will often provide a significant margin of safety. Such a company, even assuming that it has a higher debt-equity ratio, will have relatively more time to recover from the impact of recession before defaulting on any of its obligations, than will a company whose repayments of principal are closely tied to its collections of principal. In one sense, the former company is safer than the latter as long as it is operating; but at the point of liquidation, the protection behind the creditor's funds, as measured by the ratio of its debt to shareholders' equity, is of course more favorable for the latter company. Thus, a company could be meeting its debt service obligations, but insolvent if the value of its assets were insufficient to cover its liabilities at any given point, and under this definition, it would have failed. There is no necessary direct relationship between debt-equity ratios and liquidity. Consequently, in the establishment of debt policies, both the overall relation of debt to equity and the cash flow situation need to be appraised. This requires some understanding of the risks being taken by the company.

Risk Factors. In their day-to-day operations, the managements of development finance companies are concerned with minimizing unevaluated risks. There is a significant difference between a management that takes risks without realizing it and one that takes risks knowingly. Consequently, the objective of a development finance company's management is not to eliminate or even minimize risks, but to be in a position to make a sound judgment of precisely what risks are being taken and then to make a second judgment as to whether or not it should take this degree of risk.

There are several components in an estimate of a development finance company's risk under normal circumstances.

Perhaps the key component is the ability of the staff to appraise projects. This is determined by the basic competence of the people employed, their thoroughness in evaluating investments and the effectiveness of subsequent follow-up.

A second factor in evaluating risk is determined by the clientele served by the development finance company. There is a significant difference in the competence and level of sophistication of the business community dealt with by different development finance companies. Generally, the companies servicing the larger, more established industrialists take fewer risks than those whose clients are predominantly small and unproven businessmen.

Another element is the diversity of investments; most development finance companies try to spread risks by avoiding concentrations of investment in individual firms or individual sectors of industry.

The final element concerns the company's security requirements, the possibilities for the realization of security upon liquidation, and the ethics of the business community. Although the security on a loan may appear considerable, it might prove difficult to realize it in the event of liquidation; or it might be difficult to exercise mortgage rights, due to customs or title difficulties; or a combination of circumstances might make it more costly to try to realize the security on a loan than to write it off.

These are matters which managements deal with daily in their hiring and training programs, in their policies with respect to investment, and with their practices with respect to security. In dealing with them, they are endeavoring to sharpen their ability to avoid uncalculated risk. Judgments as to their effectiveness in dealing with all these components of calculation are necessary to begin to evaluate the risks they are undertaking.

Measurement of Risks. The management of a development finance company and its creditors should have some sort of evaluation of the level of risk that they are undertaking. This is difficult for a young development finance company whose loan and investment portfolio is unseasoned. As such a company matures, however, as a larger percentage of its loan portfolio represents operating projects, and as the number of projects that it has seen through from loan disbursement to loan repayment has increased, it becomes easier to evaluate meaningfully the normal operating risks undertaken by the company.

The first and basic indicator is the default experience on loan interest and principal. This should probably be separated into two parts: one that deals with the problems of timing, resulting from optimistic forecasts, particularly during the construction stage, and another that deals with defaults due to basic difficulties in the client's operations, managerially, technically or financially. With respect to equities, the indicator is the price of the shares in the marketplace, although where the market is very thin or nonexistent, this price may be difficult to establish, or it may have little meaning.

The record of defaults on interest as well as principal payments relative to total interest and principal payments due during a given period will indicate the general lag in collections; and the total funds outstanding on those projects in default related to the total loan portfolio will give some indication of the relative soundness of the portfolio. Some of these defaults may be merely temporary, with little risk of ultimate loss, whereas others will indicate more serious situations that might involve write-offs. When a development finance company has established a record of operation over ten years or so, and if its management has been realistic in recognizing the cases that are likely to be permanent defaults (even before it is appropriate to write them off), some general observations can be made as to the probable element of loss under normal operating circumstances. Finally, when it is necessary to exercise security provisions, their effectiveness can be evaluated. A similar, continuous evaluation can be made for the equity portfolio.

The difficulty is that although defaults, write-offs, and security recoveries are critical indicators, they are not popular statistics to deal with, with the result that they may not be handled in a way that makes them easy to analyze and evaluate by either management or creditors. The sensitivity of this area, however, is such that it should receive careful attention from management, particularly if management is interested in securing higher debt-equity ratios. A mature institution should be able to have a fairly clear idea of four parameters with respect to its loan and equity portfolio:

(1) the percentage of payments of interest and principal that is due during a given period, but is unpaid;
(2) the percentage of the loan portfolio that at any given time is likely to be in permanent default;
(3) the percentage of uncollectibles that is likely to be recovered as a result of security provisions;
(4) the value of the equity portfolio relative to its cost.

If these basic parameters of risk can be established under normal operating conditions, the problem becomes one of evaluating divergences from the normal risk. In practice this would mean trying to predict what would happen in business downturns. Experience in such situations is slim, but if debt-equity policy decisions are to be rational, some thought must be given to what would happen in such a situation. The following questions need to be asked. What percentage of the loan and equity portfolios would be in trouble in an expected recession? Of the projects in difficulty during a recession, what proportion could, given time, be revived? What part of the portfolio would be a complete loss and would have to be written off? Finally, of the part of the loan portfolio that must be written off, what could the development finance company hope to realize from its security? These questions, when related to cash-flow projections, can be helpful in determining whether a company is facing excessive risks of defaulting on its own obligations.

On the other hand, if, at any time, the value of a development finance company's assets is less than its liabilities, the company could theoretically be considered insolvent even though not defaulting on a cash basis. If this were viewed as a temporary situation, that is, if the company could recover itself before running into a cash deficiency, creditors would be wise to ride it out. Nevertheless, if a company's portfolio is valued at less than an amount sufficient to cover its debt, and there were some uncertainty about the future condition of the portfolio, the company would be in a serious situation, regardless of its cash flow. Thus creditors should not lose sight of the ratio of all the debt incurred by a development finance company relative to its equity, regardless of its ranking, and should insist on a ratio which provides a cushion large enough to minimize the possibility that a development bank's assets might be inadequate to cover all its liabilities, senior or junior.

Thus creditors, like shareholders themselves, are concerned with the ratio of all debt to equity. All who are involved with a development finance company would be displeased should it find it necessary to default on any of its commitments. Even if subordinated debt is available *ad infinitum*, it would be prudent to maintain a balance between debt and equity which minimizes the risk of default to *any* of the company's creditors. Hence decisions on the debt-equity ratio should be based on a systematic and continuing evaluation of the risks in the company's portfolio and of its cash flow.

Summary

Decision making on the relative amounts of conventional debt, subordinated debt, and equity in the capital structure of a development finance company has little experience to fall back on. The initial capital structures designed for many of the development finance companies associated with the World Bank were more or less taken as given. It has so far been a successful model to the extent that there does not yet appear to have been any excessive risks taken either by shareholders or by creditors. However, as companies reach their initial borrowing limits, there are forces at work which will lead to a desire on the part of the shareholders to maximize leverage and new decisions are required.

During this process the debt limits established by the World Bank have become quite widely accepted standards. However, in many cases these ratios do not indicate the real leverage on shareholders' capital, which is the critical ratio both as far as profitability is concerned and also as far as the risk position of the company's creditors is concerned. Now that original borrowing limits have been reached for a number of development finance companies, more careful thought will have to be given to an evaluation of the risks involved in doing the type of business they are doing in the environments in which they are located, in order to establish more precisely the risk position of creditors so that their decision making will be better informed. In doing this, it is necessary to analyze the cash flows of development finance companies and the quality of their portfolios as well as the underlying cushion of equity which should be required to maintain the value of assets at a level at least equal to its debts in business downturns.

IV. POLICIES REGARDING RESERVES AND RISK PROVISION

Types of Reserves

In discussing the financial policies of private development finance companies, the term "reserves" is often used in a generic sense. When so used, reserves are always considered important and "good," a sign of success; and it is commonly recommended that they be built up to the greatest extent possible. The rationale behind this, however, is sometimes unclear or at least unexplained. The word implies an extra cushion for shareholders as well as for creditors, and therefore has a positive connotation. This is indeed true to a large extent, because the accumulation of what are generally referred to as reserves indirectly implies a profitable operation as well as abstemiousness on the part of the company's shareholders, which is a reflection of their willingness to continue and to increase their investment in the company. Reserves of the type that development finance companies have in mind are also an indication that the company's equity base has been enlarged and that this has been done over and above the shareholders' requirements for cash returns on their equity.

On the other hand, there is a mystique about development finance company reserves, which sometimes endows them with greater importance in the eyes of shareholders and creditors than they in fact have in the basic financial condition of the company. In order to establish an appropriate reserve policy for a development finance company, it is necessary, first, to be precise in definition and terminology, and second, to take a hard look at different types of reserves, at their purposes and at how these purposes coincide with the objectives of a particular company.

The term "reserves" often means different things to different people. Sometimes it is used to refer to the retention of earnings and accumulated profits after *all* other charges against income have been levied, including the payment of taxes and distribution of dividends. (A part of this retention may be labeled a "legal reserve," since many countries require that a certain percentage of net profits be so retained; but this still basically represents an increase of the shareholders' equity in the company and is so indicated on its balance sheet.) These are earnings that are kept in the company, thereby increasing its net worth. If the term "reserves" is used to represent funds generated out of the true net profits of the company, then a clearer term than "reserves" would be "retained earnings." The simple word "reserves" implies something "extra" and this is not necessarily the case.

On the other hand, an entirely different type of "reserve" is the allocation of funds to cover a specific risk. There is some confusion about what such provisions are, how to provide for them, if, in fact, they are different from retained earnings, and whether a development finance company need be concerned with them at all. Often this type of "reserve," which is a provision against risk, is used interchangeably with the "reserves" described in the preceding paragraph, i.e., with "retained earnings." Yet these two financial accounts are quite different. Part of the confusion in nomenclature arises from tax and legal requirements relating to development finance companies.

Although legal requirements must, of course, be observed and the managements of development companies will wish to maximize tax advantages, these factors are secondary to the basic decisions of prudent financial policy and they should not be allowed to distort the underlying financial condition and objectives of the company. Consider, for example, an industrial concern that, under the tax code, is able to depreciate equipment at a much faster rate than the actual economic rate, thereby improving its tax position. That company will want to take advantage of this privilege. However, it will also recognize that such a depreciation is an accounting device that does not truly reflect the actual operations of the company and it will want to keep in view a realistic evaluation of assets at all times. Thus, in trying to define policies relating to the retention of earnings and the provision of specific protective reserves, it is best to ignore tax or legal implications in determining the basic objectives of the policies and then superimpose on these objectives the legal and tax factors.

Reserves on Protection Against Losses

Protective reserves are provisions against possible losses on loans and investments. The rationale for these provisions is that one of the real costs of operation for most development finance companies is losses on loans and equity investments. One way of handling these costs (losses) is merely to wait until the loss is definite (has been incurred) and then to charge it against that period's income.[3] Such a procedure would be suitable when write-offs are infrequent and of negligible amount.

For most development finance companies, however, it would be prudent to anticipate these costs and to level their cyclical impact by charging annually against income an amount estimated to be the annual expense of the losses. This expense should be deducted from income before the calculation of net profits and should be carried as a provision in the balance sheet in the form of a reduction in the value of the portfolio. If it is determined on a realistic basis, this provision should not be considered a part of the shareholders' equity. When a loan or investment has to be written down or written off, it is charged against this provisional account.

The real problem, however, lies in the levels to which these provisions might, in principle, be built regardless of the tax code, although it might be advantageous, from the point of view of taxes, to build them up more rapidly. In Colombia, for example, the tax code allows finance companies to provide against possible losses up to 10 per cent of their portfolios and the amounts charged to this account are tax-exempt until this level is reached. Consequently, for companies with rapidly expanding portfolios, there are times when their entire income,

---

[3] One way that such costs should *not* be handled is to write them off out of retained earnings. If this were done, these costs would never be reflected in the income statements, and profits would be overstated.

before provision for losses, can be charged to this account, thereby eliminating any tax liability at all; to take advantage of this tax provision, all earnings are so charged. From the financial point of view, however, it would probably not be correct to consider the whole amount set aside in this way as a provision against losses; certainly, a portion of it is retained earnings and should be considered part of the equity base of the company. On the other hand, it would be unsound to consider the entire provision as equity. Nevertheless, in practice it has often been the tax code that has determined the establishment of protective reserves and their size.

In countries that permit a tax free reserve as a provision against possible losses, the amounts so allowed generally range from 2 per cent to 10 per cent of portfolio. This range is quite wide. There will obviously be a great difference between the "paper" net profits of a company that charges no provision for losses against profits, and a company that charges an amount sufficient to maintain the reserve at, say, 8 per cent of the portfolio. Hence it is important to determine what is a proper provision for losses. Funds in excess of this provision should be considered equity, and deficiencies should call for reduction in the equity indicated on the balance sheet.

For relatively young companies, it is difficult to determine precisely the provisions that are advisable. All the factors influencing the level of risk need to be taken into account in fixing the size of such provisions. Managements should, as a first step, focus on the rationale of handling losses, make estimates of what they consider to be reasonable provisions, test these estimates under actual operating conditions, and adjust them in the light of experience but not in such a way that other distortions are created. What is clear is that retained earnings and provision for losses are far from synonymous and should be considered and dealt with separately.

Retention of Earnings and Dividend Payments

The General Case. Once provision for specific risks has been made along with all the other charges against the company's income, a policy must be adopted regarding the retention of earnings versus the distribution of cash dividends. Retained earnings per se do not necessarily make the capital structure basically sounder for conventional creditors nor stronger for shareholders.

Take the two following cases as examples.

	Company A	Company B
Paid-in share capital	100	100
Reserves	25	50
Net worth	125	150
Debt (4 × net worth)	500	600
Total resources	625	750

In both cases, equity backing amounts to 20 per cent of total resources so that the faster build-up of reserves of Company B has not made it relatively safer than Company A. For every unit retained, the company can borrow four more units; retention of earnings has allowed Company B to expand its overall resources faster than Company A. Similarly, the shareholders' position is not necessarily "better" in Company B than in Company A. It is true that the book value per share for the shareholders of Company B is larger than in Company A, but this may indicate merely that the shareholders of Company A have opted to take their return on investment in cash rather than in increased book values, preferring to add to the equity base by purchasing additional shares at a later date. Thus assuming that both companies want to expand continuously, the decision to retain or distribute is not so much a decision of which policy is "safer" as it is a decision concerning how the expansion of the company can best be financed. Retained earnings in these examples do not provide additional protection as long as they are considered part of the borrowing base. If they were not considered such, the overall debt-equity ratio would decline and creditors would have greater protection.

The Case of Companies with Subordinated Loans. The position is modified in the case of companies with subordinated loans. There are three levels of subordination, so far as loans to development finance companies are concerned: (1) loans subordinate to paid-in share capital, (2) loans ranking pari passu with paid-in share capital, and (3) loans subordinate to senior debt. Retention of earnings does have a "protective element" as far as subordinated lenders are concerned. Their risk is reduced as earnings are retained, due to the fact that in liquidation, the first line of defense will be the retained earnings of the company; consequently, a company with a higher level of retained earnings is a lesser risk to subordinated creditors than a company with relatively lower retained earnings, other things being equal. As far as conventional creditors are concerned, as long as the ratio of their loans to equity and junior debt to their loans remains fixed, and the company maintains its debt at the maximum level allowed, the retention of earnings does not affect their basic exposure.

It is thus the subordinated creditors who should normally have a special interest in the retention-of-earnings policies of their debtors. In practice, however, they have not often concerned themselves greatly with these policies and the question of retained earnings versus dividend distributions has been left to the development finance companies and the World Bank Group.

Guidelines for a Pay-Out Ratio. The policies of any company, including any development finance company, regarding retained earnings and dividends, are determined by a number of forces, some psychological and some financial. In theory, and assuming no tax, the decision to retain or distribute earnings should be determined by the rate of return on reinvested earnings as compared with the return shareholders could earn elsewhere on these funds, if they were paid-out in the form of dividends. Where shareholders are taxed on their dividend receipts, this formula would be modified; by retaining earnings, the company puts more cash to work for the investor than if he draws it out as a dividend and pays tax on it. Thus, conceivably, shareholders' financial interests might be maximized by a non-dividend policy, with all profits taken in the form of capital gains.

This procedure is, however, highly theoretical, and dividend policies are greatly influenced by a number of other factors. This is true particularly for a development finance company, since many investors in these companies are not investing purely for the financial returns. Yet even if they were, and it could be shown that full retention of earnings would maximize the returns on their investment, there would be strong pressures to pay regular dividends. First of all, over and above earnings-per-share performance, investors normally seem to value a cash income. Regular dividend payments are visible evidence of a profitable operation and may be an important determinant of the interest in, and the price paid for, the shares of a development finance company. Investors in the shares of financial institutions will be interested in the certainty of earnings and thus the dividend yield will be an important factor for them. In fact, the managements of many development finance companies use the dividend yields of other financial institutions, and even the return on fixed interest securities, as criteria for establishing the level of dividends their own companies should try to pay.

It is impossible to lay down precise rules for an appropriate pay-out ratio (dividends-to-net-profit). A common rule of thumb is that the retention of earnings will be at a reasonable rate, if about half of profits is paid in dividends. Yet in fact it is difficult to say that the pay-out ratio should be 30 per cent or 50 per cent or 70 per cent. Much depends on the situation and environment of a particular company and on whether and how it wants to finance additional growth. In normal operating conditions, the earnings of a development finance company are more predictable than are those of most industrial firms; thus, if stability of dividends is an important consideration, a development finance company could possibly have a higher pay-out ratio than an industrial firm, without undue risk of having to reduce its dividend. However, if the company's objective is to expand its equity base, then it must decide whether to pay out or to retain in the light of how best to achieve this objective. If shareholders value dividends, and will subscribe to additional shares if the dividend policy is generous, then a good argument could be made for a relatively high pay-out ratio. If the company feels that market conditions are such that the flotation of additional shares would be difficult, then it is likely to want to retain relatively more of its earnings to finance expansion. Thus a conservative dividend policy may or may not be the most effective way of increasing the equity of the company.

Aside from considerations of financing future growth, some development finance companies feel restricted in their dividend policies because they sense that, if dividends seem too attractive, the company will invite criticism from the government, particularly if the government has given significant concessions to the company. There could indeed be a basis for government criticism if dividend policy were directed toward reducing the shareholders' stake in the firm rather than toward encouraging investment in subsequent share issues. But if such criticism is based *only* on the fact that the dividends appear generous, it may be ill-founded, for the distribution or retention of earnings is not in itself the best profit indicator. Profits before distribution is the first criterion upon which the government should base its views. Two companies can have precisely the same level of profitability, yet one retain all its earnings and the other distribute all its earnings. The former is not necessarily the sounder and more responsible company, a fact which the management of a development finance company may have some difficulty in getting across.

Ultimately the stronger the performance of a development finance company, the less it will have to rely on long-term concessions. Such concessions as it may have were given in the first place in order to make the company profitable. If these concessions were too generous and resulted in "excess" profitability for the private shareholders, there would be good cause for encouraging the company to stand more on its own. The criterion for such a judgment, however, should not be the company's dividend policy, but rather the profitability of the company and the objectives of its dividend policy.

Another factor affecting dividend policies is the reluctance of companies to reduce dividends because such action is likely to have an adverse effect on investors' attitudes, regardless of the real financial situation behind the decision. For this reason managements are also unlikely to increase a dividend if maintaining the new rate might be difficult. One way of dealing with this consideration is to pay a basic dividend plus an extra dividend, the former representing the normal dividend and the latter representing a fluctuating element related to movements in profitability. Also, issuing bonus shares, by capitalizing earnings, is one way of making a non-cash payment to shareholders which has sometimes been effective. This is, however, clearly a paper transaction; and if the cash dividend rate is to be maintained, a bonus share issue only postpones an increase in the actual cash distributions, since dividends will have to be paid on a larger number of shares in the future.

A final consideration arises when a development finance company is operating in an environment in which there is a risk of devaluation. Even here, it is not possible to say with assurance that the company's shareholders will be better protected by a relatively high retention of earnings. All depends on what the shareholder would have done with his dividends had they been distributed, as compared with their effective return when reinvested in the company's operations.

Uses of Retained Earnings. There are usually no restrictions on the use of retained earnings by development finance companies. Some financial institutions, however, are required to invest all retained earnings in short-term liquid assets. Such a limitation has two effects on the financial position of a company. First, it increases the company's liquidity. Second, it reduces the risks in the overall portfolio for shareholders and creditors alike; for, with this higher liquidity, a smaller proportion of the company's assets is held in long-term risk investments.

Because retained earnings have an opportunity cost that probably approaches the cost of new equity capital, such a policy would discourage shareholders, since it would require them to make relatively high-cost equity available for low-yield short-term securities.

A restriction on the use of retained earnings is probably not a very useful policy. If such a restriction were desirable in order to increase liquidity and to reduce risk, these objectives would probably be better served by requiring a sound liquidity ratio, independent of the level of retained earnings, and by lowering the overall allowable debt-equity ratio, which is the point at which the riskiness of the company's capital structure can be most effectively evaluated and controlled.

Summary

What is generically referred to as reserve policies needs to be considered in two distinct categories: provisions for losses, which is an expense item, and retention of earnings, as opposed to distribution of net profits. Tax and legal considerations will, of course, affect what is actually done but these requirements should not distort the real economic condition or objectives of the company. Losses for most development finance companies are a cost of doing business, and orderly provision should be made for expensing these costs. The actual magnitude of provisions for losses is a matter of judgment which can be made only on the basis of experience and of a thoughtful evaluation of the risks being undertaken by a given development finance company.

To the extent that retained earnings are used as a base for additional borrowing, they should not be considered *a priori* as strengthening the company's capital structure. Such retentions are an enlargement of the capital base of the company and in this sense are similar to increases in the paid-in share capital. The decision as to the relative amounts of dividends and retentions should be based on a consideration of the shareholders' interests as well as of how the expansion of the company can most effectively be achieved. This makes rules of thumb regarding appropriate pay-out ratios quite tenuous.

V. THE INFLUENCE OF TAXATION ON THE FINANCIAL POLICY OF DEVELOPMENT INSTITUTIONS

Main Types of Taxation

Taxation is, of course, a very important element in the operation of a development finance company. It can also be a complicated one. Because of the great diversity in national tax procedures and policies, it is extremely difficult to compare the experience of one country with that of another and to generalize about the impact of taxation on the operations of their development finance companies.

The rate of taxation among the companies associated with the World Bank Group differs widely. To illustrate the range, the Industrial Finance Corporation of Thailand, for example, is completely exempt from all taxes. In India, ICICI is subject to an effective tax rate of 45 per cent on its interest and dividend income and a 30 per cent tax on capital gains. It receives no tax advantages for building provisions against losses. In addition, ICICI shareholders pay their normal rate of personal income tax on dividends distributed by the company.

There are also important differences in the level at which taxes are imposed. For instance, the first level of taxes imposed on a company usually comprises relatively small business and stamp taxes. These may, however, become quite important, as in the case of the China Development Corporation, which pays a business tax of 3.9 per cent on its gross income. Although the corporate income tax rate in Taiwan, at 18 per cent, may appear low in comparison with that of other countries, the business tax modifies this picture significantly. The next level of tax is normally that levied on the company's income. Here the rate is not the only factor of significance; not less so is the base on which the tax is computed. For example, how are the dividends received and the capital gains realized by the development finance company taxed? Are there different rates depending on whether it distributes or retains its earnings? Are deductions allowed, such as for provision against possible losses, before the computation of the income tax? A third level of taxation, which is closest to the shareholder, is the tax for which he is personally liable. Is the dividend that he receives from the company subject to personal income tax or to some other tax? Does he receive a credit for taxes paid by the company? Are the capital gains he might realize from the sale of his shares taxable, and at what rate?

The Influence of Tax Policies on Operations

Taxes will have an important influence on the policies of a development finance company. As already noted, the size of provisions against possible losses will be heavily influenced by taxation. The taxation of dividends and capital gains will have a negative, neutral or positive effect on a company's willingness to invest in equities rather than straight loans. Tax on interest received from short-term investments will affect the level of liquidity sought by the company as well as the types of securities it holds.

It is impossible to generalize about how development finance companies should be taxed. One must analyze a specific situation to see if a given tax treatment is the most efficient from every angle. There is, however, one general question that is important. Given a country's tax policies and practices, should a development finance company be treated differently from other companies, and if so, how should it be treated? If an argument were made for treating the development finance company differently from other companies,[4] it would have to be based either on a need to improve the company's after-tax profitability, or on a desire to encourage certain activities of the development company by making them more worthwhile than alternative activities.

Taxation and Profitability. The objective of after-tax profitability is related to the question of the level of incentives necessary to assure effective operation of a development finance company and the most efficient way of providing those incentives. The original premise of any incentive given to a development finance company is that special treatment is justified by the corollary benefits to the economy as a whole derived from the company's existence and operations. The question then arises as to the level of incentives which is necessary. Both for those who provide the incentives and for the shareholders of the company, the objective ought to be to keep the incentive at the lowest level conducive to sound operations. If

---

[4] There might be cases where an argument could be made for changing tax policies toward *all* companies.

some form of incentive or concession is justified, in the opinions both of government and of shareholders, it does not follow that tax relief is necessary. Other devices are available, such as cheap, long-term, subordinated loans. Tax concessions might be as valuable and effective as a subordinated loan, or even more so. Yet a general argument that development finance companies should receive tax concessions because they are promoting economic development and in effect helping to broaden the tax base is not sufficient until some judgments are made with respect to the necessity and justification for such concessions in the interest of the profitable operation of the company.

Taxation and Operations. The second justification for tax concession is to make some types of activity more attractive than others and thus to encourage them. To this end, one must consider, first, whether the existing tax code, given the relative before-tax return on interest income and on dividends, encourages one type of operation as opposed to another and, second, whether there are clear reasons for modifying the tax. It is not possible to argue that development banks should be relieved of a capital gains tax because such a tax discourages them from making equity investments. It may be that even with a capital gains tax there is an incentive to invest in equities, or that even without the tax the earnings expectation from equities is inadequate to generate much interest in equities. From a private company's point of view, of course, no tax is always preferable to some tax, but that is not the question. The tax treatment of capital gains will also affect the policies of a development company in revolving its equity portfolio. In Spain, for example, the longer an industrial bank holds a share, the higher the rate of taxation that is levied on the capital gains resulting from the sale of that share.

Finally, from the point of view of the shareholder, the treatment of dividend income and capital gains from his investment in the company will be an important factor influencing the companies' policies towards paying dividends, retaining profits, and financing the growth of the company. If it is advantageous for shareholders to realize earnings by way of capital gains rather than by way of dividend income, they (and the company) will tend to prefer that the company's earnings be retained rather than paid out as dividends. If there is a tax advantage in dividend income, there will be an incentive to finance the growth of the company by larger dividend distributions and periodic share increases.

Taxation is also an important consideration for a development finance company that is trying to raise money in its local capital market. When a government provides local currency funds, the government is acting as an intermediary, channeling the country's savings to the development bank. However, it may not be possible or practicable to obtain loans from the government and the development finance company may enter the market directly as a financial intermediary between savers and investors. The company must then try to raise funds through the sale of its own securities and this often poses a problem because of inadequate margins between the interest rate that the company will have to pay for funds and the rate at which it can lend, which in some cases may be fixed by other than market considerations. In such a case, the company's ability to raise funds can be enhanced by making the interest income from its bonds partially or completely tax-free to the bondholder. The government will have to consider how it wishes to channel the available savings and where the development finance company stands in the priorities established by the government. There is no doubt that tax exemptions of this kind can be very useful to the development bank; if it is doing an effective job, its bargaining power for attaining such concessions will be strengthened.

VI. INTEREST SPREADS

The two final variables which together determine the profitability of a development finance company (as measured by the return on net worth) are the ratio of "outside" funds to shareholders' equity and the average margin on resources employed. For most development finance companies associated with the World Bank Group, particularly the more mature ones, the largest components in the profit and loss statements are interest income on loans and debentures, administrative costs, and financial charges. These effectively determine the average margins earned by the companies. Unfortunately, management controls these elements only to a very limited extent.

As for interest rates, in some cases governments prescribe the interest rate structure, and this must be observed by the company even though market conditions might indicate different rates. Even where no rate structure is set by government, the company may be under strong pressure to charge "reasonable" rates. Sometimes the existing structure of commercial bank rates will more or less determine the company's lending rate. Whatever the determinants, in most of the countries with development banks of the World Bank Group, the companies' lending rate is in the range of 7 per cent to 9 per cent and within this range 8 per cent and 8½ per cent are by far the most common rates.

It is important to remember that factors other than interest spread also affect the gross margin earned on a development finance company's resources. At all times, but particularly in the early years of a development finance company's life, it is likely to have a considerable amount of current assets. Careful investment of these assets can make a considerable difference in the overall margin earned by the company. The return on equities can also be an important factor in the earnings of a development finance company, and should be kept in mind when interest spreads and earnings margins are being discussed. Investment-related activities such as underwriting, putting together of projects, and other services connected with lending and investment operations can be additional important sources of income.

Of the three determinants of net spreads, administrative costs are probably the most directly controllable by the management, although they too are heavily influenced by other factors, such as the nature of the company's clients, local wage levels and expatriate staff requirements. Even so, there is doubtless much that a cost-conscious management can accomplish in controlling administrative expenses. Among the companies associated with the World Bank Group that have been in operation for five or more years, administrative expenses ranged from ½ per cent to 1½ per cent of average total resources in the fifth year of operation.

Among the determinants of average margin, perhaps the least amenable to the action of management is financial charges. Many of the companies borrow a substantial part of their resources from the World Bank or other financial institutions and pay 5–6 per cent for much of their debt. Many also had low-interest or interest-free loans from government when they began operations, but generally additional funds are not available at concessionary rates. As conventionally priced debt assumes a larger share of the company's total debt, the average cost of its resources increases. Thus the more mature companies are operating with a gross spread of only 2–3 per cent on new debt resources. This does not leave much after administrative expenses are deducted, even if, at the margin, these expenses amount to less than 1 per cent of the new resources. A narrowing average spread is, of course, a major source of pressure to relax borrowing limitations in order to increase leverage, thereby maintaining the return on the shareholders' equity.

The rigidity of the principal factors determining profitability does not relieve a development finance company of responsibility of taking such actions and options as are open to it to increase its earnings. On the expenditure side, it has a responsibility to keep them at a minimum consistent with effective operation. On the income side, a market rate should be the goal of interest rate policy; and no effort should be spared to make the most of other opportunities to increase income.

VII. CONCLUSIONS

Answers to the basic financial policy decisions facing the management of private development finance companies are not very precise. Judgment and experience are important in arriving at these decisions, but at the same time there is scope for more analytical thought in providing some basic parameters which can serve to guide the decision-making process. Rules of thumb, if used loosely, may not be very helpful, and may in fact be harmful.

In the early years of a development finance company's existence, its management will primarily be occupied with organizational and operational questions. However, as the company matures, policy questions relating to finance assume a more important role, particularly if the company is aiming toward standing on its own legs with a minimum of concessions from government. This will require rethinking past policies and in some cases a significant redefinition of them. Hopefully new policies will be made, not simply by intuition and under pressure of circumstances, but with some analytical backing. This is not an easy task, but will become the more necessary as a development finance company matures.

5

RELATIONS BETWEEN GOVERNMENTS AND DEVELOPMENT FINANCE COMPANIES

by P. M. Mathew

INTRODUCTORY NOTE

Most of the development finance companies associated with the World Bank Group have been sponsored and initially all have been financed or otherwise supported by their governments. This fact places upon them a responsibility—even if their own objectives did not—to behave in the public interest as well as in the interest of their own shareholders. It also exposes them to the dangers of political pressures, which could severely inhibit their ability to act in the interest either of the general public or of their shareholders. What course of behavior will assure a smooth relationship with government within the framework of national policy and at the same time discourage or resist misguided governmental efforts to influence selection of personnel, administration, and, most of all, particular investment decisions?

One conference participant noted, early in the discussion of this subject, the paradox that development finance companies were private institutions and yet were called upon to work for very much the same objectives as governments with respect to economic development. The companies represented at the Conference that had government help desired to maintain their independence from government, not because they did not want to work with government but because otherwise a political color might be injected into their operations thereby making them inefficient. They thought it was important to make this distinction; otherwise the government would get the impression that a development finance company enjoyed the benefits of government assistance without having a sense of responsibility to it. Secondly, even though a development finance company had to align itself with the general policies of the government, it ought not to become involved in the task of economic planning, otherwise it would become politically exposed and face interference. Thirdly, a government should not enter into unfair competition with a development finance company in regard to raising capital internally in a country. Lastly, the informal relations with government agencies were important; the development finance company could greatly influence government policy.

Underlying the discussion was the uneasy feeling that, in the words of one participant, most development finance companies were "basically quasi-governmental institutions" since, directly or indirectly, they received a substantial part of their resources from governments. One wondered whether they could long remain really private, if in fact they were private now; for in each instance the private capital and the capital received from the World Bank Group were small compared with the capital provided by government. This state of affairs was justifiable in the early years of a development finance company when it was necessary to protect an infant industry. But when would they be able to stand on their own feet and develop their independent sources of finance?

This was obviously a difficult and delicate subject. Mr. Felix Chang, President of the China Development Corporation, who led the discussion, concluded that relations with government were essentially a matter of give and take. In this continuing relationship, the development finance company had to maintain its independence. It could do so if (1) it established a condition of mutual confidence with government (which close contacts with government officials and agencies would encourage) and if (2) it worked over the years to decrease its reliance on government by building up alternative sources of finance.

I. BASIS FOR COOPERATION

Development finance companies need to cooperate more with governments than other private companies, and vice versa. Companies that have built up a close relationship with the government and governments that do not substitute interference for cooperation have found their mutual relationship rewarding and beneficial in the fulfillment of their common, as well as separate, aims.

A finance company is not entirely like other private business institutions, whose all-important goal is the profit of their shareholders and whose concern with public aims is indirect; to a development company, concern with development is a prime objective in itself. Even where there is a conflict between the demands of development and self-interest, the finance company often willingly compromises its self-interest to a degree in order to foster development.

Recognizing the concern of development banks with development and their potential for promoting development, governments have given many of them various types of assistance.

In most countries, government development finance institutions exist side by side with private ones. One of the major problems of the private companies is to evolve a *modus vivendi* with the public agencies. Unless the roles and spheres of interest of the two types of institution are defined and coordinated, competition could develop between them to the disadvantage of both and to the serious detriment of the private institutions.

Development finance companies often need close contact with governments in order to serve their clients effectively. Many developing countries use measures such as licensing and control of foreign exchange and of capital issues to regulate industry or to direct investment into desired channels. Almost all governments provide incentives and concessions in varying degrees to promote desired forms of investment. Entrepreneurs, particularly foreign investors who do not have the contacts or the ability to obtain government concessions, often rely on development banks to negotiate and insure coordinated action for the issuance of permits.

Some development companies consider the need for cooperation with the government so vital to their success and viability that they have provisions, either in their charters or in their statements of general policy, requiring them so to cooperate. In some cases, these provisions have been suggested by the government that provided important financial support to the companies.

II. PUBLIC ECONOMIC OBJECTIVES

Like other private businesses, development finance companies live within the economic climate of their respective countries and are affected by it. Rarely do they assert their private nature to the extent of pursuing policies in opposition to government aims, but they often work closely with governments in evolving the economic climate and the government policies that influence it.

With a view to quickening the pace of economic growth, many governments draw up economic development plans and programs. Even where these primarily concern government investment outlays, they almost invariably lay down private investment goals and propose public policies aimed at facilitating their achievement. Areas of priority are often indicated and incentives are offered. To what extent should a private development finance company become involved in shaping these targets and policies?

Development companies generally feel that too close an association with the government's planning machinery, which might involve them in responsibility for formulating government plans, is not one of the company's normal objectives. Many consider that too close an association with government thinking may result in their identification in the public mind with the government. In some countries, such an identification is enough to discourage prospective clients. Moreover, excessive preoccupation with economic development might conflict with the company's duty to its shareholders to invest its resources, including staff time, to the best corporate advantage. A development company has to marry its financing function and its development function, and the marriage should not be an unequal one.

Operating, as they do, at the core of the industrialization process, finance companies often acquire an intimate knowledge of the effects of government measures and policies on industrial investment, and are among the best sources of objective judgment about their soundness. They are also often the best informed agency in the private sector on the problems of industry. These advantages enable the companies to offer sound advice to governments and to have their advice taken seriously. It is not, therefore, surprising that the management and staff of development companies find themselves invited to sit on government committees concerned with public policy and plans. If kept within reasonable bounds, this association is of mutual benefit. It gives the finance company important contacts, as well as an insight into government motivations and aims for the future. It enables the company not only to influence climate, but also to acclimatize itself better to its environment and to make the best of it. On the other side, it enables the government to feel the pulse of the private industrial sector and to know in what way, and in what sectors, private resources are likely to be applied to development.

In the course of a study of its country's sugar industry, for example, one of the development companies found that existing government policies had the effect of driving the industry to virtual bankruptcy. The finance company proposed appropriate policy changes to the government; these the government accepted. The result was a spectacular recovery of the industry and new business for the finance company.

Many development companies consider formal statements of the country's investment programs and economic development plans very useful. These documents enable them to decide whether their own projects contribute to the country's sound economic development. Few among them would like to make an investment that they cannot so justify. If government policies are enforced through such administrative devices as licensing, exchange allocations and capital issue controls, the decision that a project has priority is ready-made in advance for the finance companies to act on.

Will too close an association with policy making commit a development bank to implement government programs, even if such a course is not in its own interest? Will management and staff become missionaries, losing the cautious and critical attitude essential for a banker? Will the company tend to neglect its primary function of financing, in the exhilaration of finding itself in the highest councils of the land? These are legitimate questions that worry some development finance companies and point up the dangers of carrying contacts to excess. Caution and sound judgment are necessary.

III. GOVERNMENT ASSISTANCE

All but two of the twenty-five[1] privately or predominantly privately-owned development companies with which the World Bank family is associated are under obligation to their respective governments or its agencies for important assistance in one form or another. Nineteen of these companies have public funds in their share capital, ranging from 4 per cent to 44 per cent. Fourteen have received loans on favorable terms, with long terms and grace periods, bearing little or no interest, and ranking equal or subordinate to share capital. The amount of these loans varies from two-thirds to seven times the original share capital.

Twenty of the twenty-five companies depend on loans from the government or its agencies or on discounting facilities with central banks for most or some of their local currency resources. Nineteen of them, which have received World Bank loans, have obtained government guarantees to cover the loans. Governments have also guaranteed loans by foreign governments to some of the companies. In many cases, the proportion of their funds derived independently of the government is small indeed, relative to total resources.

Governments have supplied two of these companies with funds to manage for investment or reinvestment purposes, the amount ranging as high as 38 per cent of the total portfolio of one company. In another, the ratio reached 50 per cent until recently, when most of it was converted to a subordinated loan. One company also draws upon a public fund created for the special purpose of making equity investments for increasing domestic participation in enterprise.

Governments have made it possible for several companies to obtain technical assistance free of cost or at reduced cost from friendly governments and international agencies. Eleven

[1] As of June 30, 1967.

companies enjoy favorable tax treatment, either as a concession to each one individually, or to development finance companies generally; four companies are completely exempt from taxes on income earned and dividends paid.

To many of these companies, governments are an important or perhaps the only potential source of fresh domestic capital. To the government, they are important tools in the developmental effort. Are these institutions really private? To what extent are they subject to government influence? Is some measure of government influence justified? Where should one draw the line?

IV. GOVERNMENT INFLUENCE

There can be no consensus as to what it is legitimate for a government to do vis-à-vis the private sector, in view of the differences in political systems, public aims and administrative traditions. Industrial licensing, exchange controls, interest rate restrictions and the like might be obnoxious in one country, but normal in another. Partnership with government might be frowned upon in one country, but welcome in another. What is legitimate government influence on a development finance company in a given country will depend on what is, on the whole, accepted by the private sector in that country as the normal role for government in the economy.

In view of the common interest of the government and the development bank in economic development, the government is likely to influence the company in achieving public goals. For example, a government may believe that cheap credit is an essential instrument for rapid growth and may try, by regulation or more often through persuasion, to inhibit the finance company's freedom to charge an interest rate that the market will bear. Especially where the government has provided the finance company with cheap funds or facilitated the channeling of such funds into the company, it may feel that the company should limit itself to something below the market rate rather than the maximum possible rate. In some countries, a market rate for long-term funds other than that set by the finance company does not exist.

Restrictive government policies applied to interest rates can have a significant effect on the earnings of a development bank. It may be justified in charging something higher for its long-term financing than the prevailing commercial bank rate for short-term advances, but partly in deference to a government's expressed or anticipated wishes and partly because of its loyalty to the cause of development, it rarely charges rates equal to the best it can get. Some finance companies feel inhibited in undertaking the risks they are designed to take because they do not feel that they have the freedom to charge a price commensurate with the risk. Quite different is the case of one government, itself in the long-term lending business through public agencies, which persuaded a large private development finance company to increase its rates in line with an increase in government rates. The fact that most companies have contented themselves with a somewhat lower rate than the prevailing commercial rate, and have not protested too loudly against government pressures to keep rates low, might be taken to mean that, within bounds, they consider government influence on interest rates legitimate. It also probably indicates a responsible attitude on the part of most governments, which refrain from pushing a development company too hard in the direction of rates that are too low.

Some development companies are under pressure from governments to finance small scale enterprise. Because of the high cost of investigating and supervising small projects, and because of a feeling that small loans are riskier, most finance companies shy away from small loans. In many countries there are special financial and promotional agencies to assist small enterprises. Typically, they are public and provide financing on concessional terms.

Pressure on development banks to involve themselves with small loans stems from various causes. Governments sometimes are unable to raise funds to support small enterprises; and, if they have financed private development finance companies, they may ask them to set apart some of their funds for small enterprises, on lenient terms.

Because of the paucity of local entrepreneurs and capital in many developing countries, industry is dominated by foreigners. Nationals engage only in small business. Due to national sentiment, development finance companies feel obliged to assist local entrepreneurs, and an effective way to help them is by assisting small enterprises. Noting that much of the resources of private development companies is used to assist foreign-sponsored businesses, governments sometimes feel it desirable to ask the companies to interest themselves in supporting domestic entrepreneurs.

Similar to the financing of small enterprise is the financing of the less developed regions of a country. Most governments have the avowed purpose of quickening the growth of such districts, and they devote public funds to the necessary promotional effort. Industries for such regions may not be attractive for private investors without special guarantees. They are also unattractive to a development finance company, except on special terms. Finance companies may be under pressure to assist such projects, particularly if they have themselves received government assistance. At least one finance company, which has to cooperate with the government's plans to offer low interest rates in an underdeveloped region, has arrangements with the government to be compensated for the differential between the company's normal rates and the rate desired by the government. Depending on the circumstances, a measure of flexibility on the part of the development company in assisting such projects may result in a better alternative to the economy than the only other one usually available, namely, for the enterprise to be fully government-financed.

When development finance companies are called upon to undertake risky or unprofitable projects at the suggestion of the government, it is normal for them to expect compensation. Otherwise, they would be acting under duress and against their own interest. Some governments, however, have argued that if the companies have already received special governmental assistance in the form of low-cost, subordinated funds, it is their duty to finance the uneconomic and risky schemes in which the government is interested.

When granting financing and assistance to development companies, the government rarely intends to require in return that the companies undertake particular forms of uneconomic financing. Often the government is more likely to have based its concessions on the prospect of the general benefits to the economy from the assistance that the finance company was designed to provide. In some cases, the government's financing of a private development bank has reflected its failure to achieve certain results on its own. In these circumstances, the company is entitled to take for granted that governmental assistance will be available for all the kinds of operation envisaged when the funds were provided, and not for specific programs needing subsidy and identified only later. Finance companies would therefore be justified in assuming that if governments expect them to undertake, in the public interest, specific risks that are not normal to their operations, adequate compensation should be forthcoming. The compensation may take the form of an interest subsidy, a guarantee of the investment, or a promise by the government to buy the investment on pre-agreed terms.

The government's invitation to finance companies to branch out into areas or lines of activity beyond those originally contemplated may be flattering, but many companies prefer to be cautious and avoid undue risks, although they are willing to expand their role in response to their commitment to the developmental effort.

Finance companies using public funds sometimes receive requests for information from governments, in response to questions posed in parliament or by legislative committees. Most companies recognize that it is only legitimate that the government, having invested public funds in them, be in a position to account for the end-use of those funds, and they are therefore ready to supply the information. It is also proper, within limits, for a government to examine the operations and creditworthiness of a company in some detail before deciding to grant it assistance. It is generally agreed, however, that if supplying the information were to violate a client's confidence, the company would be justified in withholding the information.

Discussion in legislatures exposes finance companies to public criticism, without an opportunity to defend themselves. Most companies shun such publicity. At its worst, such a discussion can deteriorate into an occasion for officials and politicians to apply pressure on the company to act against its best judgment, or to reap public revenge for favors refused.

V. GOVERNMENT INTERFERENCE

Most finance companies clearly recognize the line of separation between cooperation and interference. The government may seek the cooperation of a finance company in furthering its public aims, such as implementing government priorities for channeling investment, assisting particular sectors like small industry, giving special attention to projects sponsored by nationals, developing the technical and managerial skills of nationals, taking an interest in industrial promotion and attracting foreign investment. In fact, in countries where the government controls many sectors of the economy, such cooperation is essential and in the interest of the finance company. Interference begins when the government goes beyond the general area of these policies and tries to influence or control the finance company's decisions with respect to internal administration, staffing and investments.

The general experience of finance companies is that they have been able to develop a cooperative relationship with the government without inviting interference, but there are a few instances of governmental attempts to influence decisions.

It is useful to distinguish between interference by the government, acting as a public body, and interference by individual members of the government, acting in their personal capacity. The former is often born of respectable motives. The government should, nevertheless, recognize the harm it can do by trying to impose its will on a company in matters that are strictly within the company's private domain.

Most often, interference arises from a feeling on the part of governments that since they contributed substantially to the resources of the finance companies, and were, in some cases, also the sponsors, they are entitled to take a close interest in all of the company's affairs. When domestic private ownership of the company is small and the government is the substitute therefor, and when foreign participation is large, governments seem to feel a special responsibility for keeping watch over and guiding the affairs of the finance company. Whatever the apparent justification, interference can, in the long run, do only harm.

When a finance company seeks a participation in its share capital or other benefits from the government, the company's relations with the government are often discussed in great detail. When interference occurs, it is often because the government has lost sight of the relationship envisaged when the company was established. If, as has happened on rare occasions, governments were to treat private development finance companies as private only in form and as public corporations in reality, they would destroy the very basis on which the companies were founded, thereby undermining their effectiveness and usefulness.

Wise governments recognize that there are bound to be some differences in approach between them and the finance companies. They do not ask for conformity, but only for intelligent decisions that take into account the public interest as the government's representative explains it to the company. Wise finance companies have learned to respect the government's views; but they also realize that, if they were not to preserve their independence in decision making, they would be selling out their character as a private agency.

The type of interference that finance companies resent and resist as best they can originates with individual officials. Resort to this, backed up with veiled or open threats of dire consequences, has the purpose of securing for officials' friends special and undeserved favors. Except in countries where corruption is so extensive as to be open, this type of interference seldom comes to the surface, but it has occasionally posed serious problems.

VI. THE GOVERNMENT DIRECTOR

Financial assistance, either as share capital or as loans to a finance company, often obligates the company to have on its board one or more directors representing the government. In the interest of coordinating the development bank's activities with public agencies responsible for investment or technical assistance, such agencies also may be represented on the board of the finance company, and vice versa. The government directors are an obvious and, to a certain extent, legitimate channel of government influence.

The role of a director of a finance company representing the government is threefold. In his personal capacity, he contributes to the company his general vision, experience, and judgment. As the representative of his government, he makes sure that the company has correctly understood the government's developmental aims and policies. Again, as a government nominee, the director is often the channel through which the company sounds out and formally approaches the government when it needs a government ruling either for itself or for a client.

In addition to supplying the government director with normal information to which directors are entitled, companies are often obligated under loan contracts to supply the government with other specific information about their operations.

Because of the sensitivity of some of their clients, some private development companies have been troubled about the extent of the information to be given the government. Clients sometimes fear that information supplied by them to the finance company will end up, via the government director, on the tax collector's desk. As a rule, however, managements do not feel seriously inhibited on this score.

Some finance companies believe that the presence of a government official on the company's board provides a point of too frequent contact with, and too close involvement of the government in, the company's affairs. For this reason, they would prefer to avoid government representation on their boards. The extent of this feeling varies with the degree of the government's involvement in industrial and related sectors. In some newly independent countries, government participation and representation on the boards of finance companies, as well as in industrial enterprises, are often welcomed by the domestic as well as the foreign private sector as a factor in the stability of their investment.

VII. RELATIONSHIP WITH PUBLIC FINANCIAL AGENCIES

Reference has already been made to the need for coordination between the activities of private development finance companies, on the one hand, and of public financial and other related agencies, on the other. Where there is no coordination, a public financial agency could compete unfairly with a private company by applying inadequate standards of judgment to the soundness of projects seeking assistance and by offering assistance at below-market rates; public agencies, which often receive capital without cost or obligation to return a profit, can afford to be more liberal than private companies. Both methods are potentially harmful to the real interests of the economy.

Industry at any cost is not necessarily better than no industry. If, as a result of inadequate appraisal, an unsound project goes ahead, it involves the economy in unnecessary costs that are often hidden. If a fundamentally viable project receives a subsidy, it unnecessarily fattens someone's purse at the expense of the taxpayer. If a project becomes viable only because of the subsidy, the economy pays a price to support an uneconomic industry. It rarely happens that both the direct and indirect benefits derived by the economy from such industries adequately compensate for the visible and invisible costs to the economy.

It is, however, reasonable to assume that some uneconomic projects will somehow be financed in most countries, not excluding the developing countries, and that some of them will be subsidized. Governments sometimes conceive prestige projects, and private entrepreneurs can almost always be found, at a price, to implement them. Political considerations, the needs of underdeveloped parts of the country, a misconceived belief in industrialization at any cost, and prospects of personal gain to public officials are among the motivations for governmental adventures with uneconomic industrial investments. Granting that the pressures to finance such projects exist, many private finance companies feel it desirable that a public financial agency be available to absorb these pressures. Where there is no such public agency or it lacks the necessary resources, a private company may be subjected to severe pressure to finance prestige projects. If the private company received government funds at little or no interest, pressure is likely to be applied also for reduced interest rates for such projects.

When it becomes an important shareholder in a finance company, the International Finance Corporation has frequently negotiated an understanding with the government about the coordination of the private company with public financial agencies. Typically, this understanding provides that the public agency will not finance any project in which the private company is interested, that it will route all investment proposals initially received by it to the private company, and that the private company will not finance projects below, nor the public agency above, a certain level. Where no formal understandings are established in advance, they inevitably evolve through a period of coexistence. The understandings also envisage joint operations of mutual advantage. Sometimes coordination is facilitated by representation for each company on the other's board.

If they have rejected projects as unsound, some private development finance companies feel that the financing of these by a public financial agency would represent unfair competition. This is perhaps an imaginary grievance. No private company can seriously complain if a project that it had had an opportunity to finance, but which it had turned down as unsound, were to end up in the government's lap. In the best of circumstances, a government's willingness to accept the findings of a private company about the soundness of a project and to desist from financing it will depend on the government's confidence in the technical ability of the staff and the judgment of the private company's management; the best of circumstances seldom exists, and it would be unrealistic to assume that governments are entirely motivated by undiluted economic criteria. The government's financing of projects that are considered unsound by private companies, the offer of below-market interest rates, and the relaxation of appraisal standards remain sources of irritation for several private finance companies.

Demarcating the fields of interest of public and private development finance institutions avoids wasteful competition. On the other hand, the development of opportunities for joint operations is constructive coexistence. Public agencies that are obliged, as agents of the government, to finance projects needing special financial arrangements could, where the projects are sound, invite private agencies to undertake senior financing at market rates, while they themselves provide junior financing on appropriate soft terms.

If the resources of the public agency are large, it will be in the interest of the private company to cultivate the former in order to use it as a source of additional financing for its own projects. In this way, the private company can reduce its exposure and the consequent risk. Some private companies have found it advantageous to associate a public agency with them in order to facilitate the granting of the various government permits that clients require.

In some countries, government promotional-cum-financing agencies finance and organize feasibility studies, which they then turn over to private finance companies to implement. If it is the private company that adopts the project, it is useful to set aside a part of the financing for the public agency concerned, in order to maintain good will.

There are several public financial agencies that have developed competent staffs with a diversity of appraisal skills. Joint operations with such agencies provide the private company with the opportunity for a double check on its own conclusions. Setting up joint appraisal teams serves to minimize the time needed to complete appraisals of projects that interest both and to amalgamate the experience of both. When it is not practicable to set up joint teams, the circulation of studies among the interested parties is being adopted as a substitute for sharing views and experience.

VIII. SAFEGUARDING INDEPENDENCE

The points of contact between the government and a development finance company are many. Every company is exposed at sometime or another to government's attempts to influence it. However, the real test of independence is not whether a company is faced with government pressure, but whether it has been able, in practice, to make its investment decisions, choose its staff and carry on its administration solely on the basis of its own best judgment. Judged by these criteria, many companies, even some in centrally run economies, are remarkably independent. This is a testimony no less to the good sense, abstemiousness and foresight of governments than it is to the strength and tact of the boards and managements of the companies themselves.

Nevertheless, safeguarding their independence, which is crucial to their effectiveness, is a matter which gives development finance companies continuous concern and calls for continuous vigilance. Many companies wish they did not have to concern themselves with this problem. But so long as they have to depend on governments for capital and other assistance, they cannot avoid exposure to governments' attempts to influence them. This dependence does not appear to be a short-term feature. The older finance companies associated with the World Bank Group, after about ten years of operation, feel that they still cannot depend to any significant extent on the market for their resources. It will probably take them another decade to be able to stand on their own legs.

In some cases, the World Bank family has been able to play a part in maintaining the independence of a development finance company. An IFC subscription to share capital, sometimes accompanied by its presence on the board of directors and almost always involving an intimate relationship, has on occasion provided a shield against government pressure. No less important has been the World Bank's insistence on operational independence as a condition for a Bank loan. The influence of the World Bank family stems not from legal arrangements but from the fact of its being a continuing, and often the most important, single source of finance for development finance companies.

The experience of the older, more effective development finance companies offers instructive guidelines for a successful relationship with government and for the avoidance of interference from government. Such a company values a close relationship with the government. It welcomes opportunities to advise the government on economic and industrial policy, serving on government committees when invited, but avoiding responsibility for public planning. It equips itself adequately through study and research to act as a responsible representative of the private sector, and scrupulously avoids giving the impression that it is an arm of the government. It uses its contacts with government agencies to the best advantage, for itself and for its clients. It gives all due information to the government, but jealously protects from exposure to public bodies the information given in confidence by its clients.

Such a company cooperates with the government as fully as it can in matters of policy, but stays at arm's length in matters of investment and administrative decisions. It builds a cooperative relationship with public agencies financing or otherwise assisting industry. To the extent it can, it joins in the promotional effort to get new industries started, to develop the capital market, to improve institutional arrangements to facilitate investment and to attract foreign investment. It does not forget that it is a developmental agency as well as a financial institution obligated to return a profit to its shareholders; and it makes a wise compromise when the two aims seem to conflict. It functions as an evolving mechanism in an evolving economy, as mindful of its responsibilities as it is watchful of its rights. When these attitudes of a finance company are matched with those of a sensible government which recognizes, despite the finance it has provided, the merit of refraining from interference and in allowing the company to act on strictly economic and financial grounds, the result is an effective private financial institution which is both a responsive and a responsible partner in the government's developmental efforts.

APPENDIX

Participants in the Conference of Development Finance Companies, October 11–13, 1965

Institution	*Name, Title, and Official Address*
Banco del Desarrollo Económico Español (BANDESCO)	Sr. José María Marzo Churruca Director General Banco del Desarrollo Económico Español Apartado de Correos 50460 Príncipe 12 Madrid, Spain
Banque Ivoirienne de Développement Industriel (BIDI)	Mr. Paul F. Blanc Managing Director Banque Invoirienne de Développement Industriel B.P. 4470 Abidjan, Ivory Coast
Banque Nationale pour le Développement Économique (BNDE)	Mr. Mohamed Benkirane Director General Banque Nationale pour le Développement Économique Boite Postale 407 Rabat, Morocco

110 APPENDIX

Institution	Name, Title, and Official Address
C.A. Venezolana de Desarrollo (CAVENDES)	Dr. Manuel Delgado Rovati General Manager C.A. Venezolana de Desarrollo Apartado 11341 Chacao, Caracas, Venezuela
China Development Corporation (CDC)	Mr. Felix S. Y. Chang President China Development Corporation 181-5 Chung Shan Road N., Section 2 Taipei, Taiwan Republic of China
Corporación Financiera de Caldas (CF CALDAS)	Dr. Guillermo Sanint Botero Vice President Corporación Financiera de Caldas Apartado Aéreo 460 Manizales, Colombia
Corporación Financiera Colombiana (CF COLOMBIANA)	Dr. Guillermo Herrera Carrizosa President Corporación Financiera Colombiana Edificio Banco de Bogotá, Carrera 10 Bogotá, Colombia
Corporación Financiera Nacional (CF NACIONAL)	Dr. José Gutierrez Gomez President Corporación Financiera Nacional Apartado Aéreo 1039 Medellín, Colombia
Industrial Credit and Investment Corporation of India Limited (ICICI)	Mr. H. T. Parekh General Manager Industrial Credit and Investment Corporation of India Limited 163 Backbay Reclamation Bombay 1, India
Industrial Development Bank of Israel Limited (IDBI)	Dr. A. Neaman Managing Director Industrial Development Bank of Israel Limited 9 Ahad Haam Street, Shalom Mayer Tower Tel Aviv, Israel
Industrial Development Bank of Turkey (TSKB)	Mr. Bahaeddin Kayalioglu Assistant General Manager Industrial Development Bank of Turkey P.O. Box 17 Karakoy Istanbul, Turkey

Institution	Name, Title, and Official Address
Industrial and Mining Development Bank of Iran (IMDBI)	Mr. A. Gasem Kheradjou Managing Director Industrial and Mining Development Bank of Iran P.O. Box 1801 Tehran, Iran
Liberian Bank for Industrial Development and Investment (LBIDI)	Mr. P. Clarence Parker General Manager Liberian Bank for Industrial Development and Investment P.O. Box 547 Monrovia, Liberia
Nigerian Industrial Development Bank Limited (NIDB)	Mr. James S. Raj, General Manager, and Mr. S. B. Daniyan, Deputy General Manager Nigerian Industrial Development Bank Limited M & K House 96/102 Broad Street P.O. Box 2357 Lagos, Nigeria
Oesterreichische Investitionskredit A.G. (IVK)	Dr. Wilhelm Teufenstein Member of the Managing Board Oesterreichische Investitionskredit A.G. Am Hof 4 Vienna 1, Austria
Pakistan Industrial Credit and Investment Corporation Limited (PICIC)	Mr. N. M. Uquaili Managing Director Pakistan Industrial Credit and Investment Corporation Limited P.O. Box 5080 Karachi, Pakistan
Private Development Corporation of the Philippines (PDCP)	Mr. Vincente R. Jayme Executive Vice President Private Development Corporation of the Philippines CBTC Building Ayala Avenue, Makati, Rizal Manila, The Philippines
Teollistamisrahasto Oy (Industrialization Fund of Finland) TR	Mr. Seppo Konttinen General Manager Teollistamisrahasto Oy (Industrialization Fund of Finland) Lonnrotinkatu 13 Helsinki, Finland

Institution	Name, Title, and Official Address
International Finance Corporation (IFC)	Mr. A. G. Arango IFC Representative on Board of CAVENDES
	Mr. John G. Beevor IFC Representative on Boards of NIDB, BNDE, TSKB
	Mr. E. T. Kuiper IFC Consultant
	Mr. Virgil C. Sullivan IFC Representative on Boards of PICIC, IFCT, MIDFL

INDEX

Absentee ownership. *See* Foreign investors
Accounting procedures:
  effects of, 32, 34, 35, 78
Administrative expenses, 89
Africa, 2, 51
Aims. *See* Goals
Analyses of cash flows, 71, 74
Appraisal of projects, 9, 49, 52, 72
  See also Feasibility studies
Asia, 51
Assessments of performance, 53
Assets:
  evaluation of, 78
  investments in, 27
Assistance from governments, 96–97
Auditing procedures:
  effects of, 32, 34, 35, 78, 100
Auditors:
  need for, 53
Austria, 2

Banco del Desarrollo Económico Español, 33
Bankers:
  responsibilities of, 7–8, 9
Banks:
  sales by, 40
Bearer shares, 35

Board of directors:
  of finance company clients, 50, 54–56
  government representatives, 102–3
Bonds, 88
Bonus shares, 83
Borrowing:
  costs of, 89–90
  lending rates, 88–89
  limits of, 62, 64, 66, 68–69, 75, 90
  power of companies, 62
  See also Debts; Loans
Brokers:
  development finance company as, 36, 42, 44
  fees for, 41
  responsibility of, 44
  role of, 39, 40
Business community. *See* Entrepreneurs
Business practices:
  effects of, 31–32
  local variations in, 10, 11, 14, 16, 51
  low standards of, 38
  opposition to changes in, 32, 37
  as risk factors, 72
  upgrading of, 34–35
  See also Entrepreneurs

Capital:
  cost of, 68
  from government, 20, 33, 66, 91–92, 96–97, 98, 99
Capital gains:
  taxation of, 31, 87
Capital market:
  stimulation of, 11, 19, 25, 27
Capital structure of companies, 62, 65–66, 79
  examples of, 69–70
Cash flow:
  evaluation of, 70–71, 74
China, 2
China Development Corporation, 85, 92
Clients:
  business practices of. *See* Business practices
  methods of gaining, 16–17
  relationship with, 49–58
  service to, 18
Collection of debts:
  lag in, 71, 73
Colombia, 2, 3, 49, 66, 78
Competition:
  among development finance companies, 17
  with public agencies, 103
Concessions given, 82, 83, 86–87, 88, 93, 96–97, 99
  minimization of, 63
Conference of Development Finance Companies, 1
Confidence:
  of investors, 36, 38, 39, 43, 81
  of managers, 54
Conflict of interest, 55, 56
Consultants:
  role of, 15–16, 53
Consumer financing:
  effects of, 30
Control of enterprises, 18
Controls in marketing:
  development of, 40
Convertible debentures, 29–30
Cooperation with government:
  basis for, 93–94
Corporación Financiera Nacional of Colombia, 49
Corporations:
  need for, 35
Costs:
  administrative, 89
  of borrowing, 89–90
  of capital, 68
  losses as, 78

  of promotional activities, 15, 21–22
  of underwriting fees, 41
Creditors:
  aims of, 64–65
Cyclical movement:
  of losses, 78
  of promotional activity, 17

Debenture issues, 40
  convertible, 29–30
  resources from, 33
Debts:
  defaults in payments of, 71, 73–74, 78
  equity related to, 59, 64–65, 66, 70–75, 80, 84
  levels of, 59
  See also Borrowing; Loans
Defaults, 71, 73–74, 78
Determinants of average margin, 88–89
Devaluation:
  risk of, 83
Development:
  facilitation of, 33
  stages in, 8–9
Development Bank of Ethiopia, 4
Directors. *See* Board of directors
Discounting facilities, 96
Distribution of wealth, 28
Diversification of investments, 37, 57, 72
Dividend payments, 60, 79–83, 87

Earnings retained, 77, 79–84, 87
Economic planning:
  by government, 20, 94–96
Entrepreneurs:
  activities of, 9, 20, 93, 98
  lack of, 51
  liaison with government planners, 14, 16
  local variations in, 10, 11, 14, 16, 51
  See also Business practices
Equity fund, 20
Equity participation, 19, 20, 22–23
  ability to raise capital for, 63
  extent of, 45–46
  and government assistance, 20, 96
  and levels of debt, 59, 64–65, 66, 70–75, 80, 84
  losses on, 71, 73, 78
  need for, 20

Ethics:
  local variations in, 31–32
Ethiopia, 4
Evaluation:
  of assets, 78
  of cash flows, 70–71, 74
  of risks, 64, 65, 70, 73–75
Execution of project, 9
Expansion of security ownership:
  by developing trading mechanisms, 35–37
  factors influencing, 28–32
  by increasing number of securities, 37–39
  methods of, 25–47, 63
  by portfolio sales, 42–43
  by public issues, 38, 39, 40
  reasons for encouragement of, 27–28
  role of development finance company in, 32–46
  by stabilization of market, 43–45
  by underwriting, 39, 40–41
  by unit trusts, 41–42
  by upgrading business practices, 34–35
Expenses. *See* Costs

Feasibility studies:
  financing of, 15, 22
  focus of, 15
  need for, 8, 10, 15–16
  See also Project
Financial policy:
  capital structure variations, 62
  debt-equity relationships, 64–76
  dividend payments, 60, 81–83, 87
  elements of problems in, 61–63
  interest spreads, 88–90
  problems of, 59–90
  reserves, 76–84
  and retention of earnings, 77, 79–84, 87
  and taxation, 85–88
  variations in objectives, 62–63
Financing:
  consumer, 30
  for feasibility studies, 15, 22
Finland, 2, 3
Follow-up investigations, 53–54
Forecasting of cash flows, 70–71, 74
Foreign investors, 11, 18, 19, 28, 32, 37, 55, 93, 98, 101
Funds:
  equity, 20
  for feasibility studies, 15, 22
  from government, 20, 33, 66, 92, 96–97, 98, 99
  for specific risks, 77, 78–79
  subordinated, 62, 66–70

Goals:
  of companies, 62–63
  of government, 94–96
  of shareholders and creditors, 64–65
Government:
  aid to small enterprises, 98
  aid to underdeveloped regions, 99
  assistance from, 20, 33, 66, 92, 96–97, 98, 99
  attitudes toward risks, 99, 100
  cooperation with, 93–94
  criticism from, 82
  directors representing, 102–3
  economic objectives of, 94–96
  influence of, 97–100
  information requested by, 100, 102–3
  and interest rates, 88–89, 97–98
  interference by, 100–2
  liaison with entrepreneurs, 14, 16
  loans by, 33
  management of funds belonging to, 62
  participations in industry, 58
  planning by, 20, 94–95
  public and private agencies, 93, 103–5
  relations with, 91–107
  safeguards for independence of finance company, 91–92, 106–7
  securities, 31, 35–36
  support of unit trust funds, 42
  uneconomic projects of, 104
  See also Concessions; Taxation
Greece, 66
Group promotion, 19
Guidelines:
  for pay-out ratio, 81–83
  in underwriting, 45–46

ICON Securities, 37, 45
Identification of projects, 8, 9
Independence of development finance company, 92, 106–7
Independent consultants, 53
India, 2, 45, 59, 69, 85
Indicators:
  of profit, 82
  of risk, 73–76

116 INDEX

Indonesia, 4
Industrial Bank of Indonesia, 4
Industrial Credit and Investment Corporation of India, 59, 69–70, 85
Industrial Development Bank of Turkey, 2, 70
Industrial Finance Corporation of Thailand, 85
Industrial Mining and Development Bank or Iran, 38
Inflation:
  effects of, 30
Information:
  need for, 53–54, 55
  supplied to government, 100, 102–3
Inspection of client enterprises, 53–54
Institutions:
  cooperation with, 39
  as investors, 30, 34
  public and private agencies, 93, 103–6
Insurance companies, 30, 39, 40
Interest:
  defaults on, 73
  government policies for rates, 88–89, 97–98
  spreads in, 60, 64, 88–90
Interference by government, 100–2
International Finance Corporation, 1, 104
Intuition:
  role of, 61, 67n
Investment capital. See Capital market
Investment yields. See Profitability
Investors:
  aims of, 64
  confidence of, 36, 38, 39, 43
  foreign, 11, 18, 19, 28, 32, 37, 55, 93, 98, 101
  institutional, 30, 34
  public, 23
Involvement:
  in governmental policy-making, 94–95
  in management of client enterprises, 56–58
  over-involvement of staff, 20–21, 23
Iran, 2, 38
Israel, 2

Joint ventures, 19, 28

Lagos Stock Exchange, 37
Legal aspects:
  effects of practices, 35
  groundwork necessary, 39
  of reserves, 77
  of security marketing, 29–30
Lending rates. See Borrowing
Leverage of finance companies, 64, 65, 66, 68, 69, 76, 90
Liberia, 2
Licensing procedures:
  development of, 40
Limits:
  of borrowing, 62, 64, 66, 68–69, 75, 90
  of equity investments, 45–46
  on retained earnings used, 83–84
Liquidity:
  importance of, 29, 35, 43, 44, 71–72, 80, 83–84
Loans:
  ability to raise capital for, 63
  from government, 33, 96
  losses on, 78
  and public issues, 37, 38
  and representations on boards, 56
  security required for, 35, 72
  small loans granted, 98
  subordinated, 62, 66–70, 80–81, 99
  See also Borrowing; Debts
Losses:
  avoidance of, 58
  in collection of debts, 71–73, 78
  cyclical impact of, 78
  provisions for, 77, 78–79

Malaysian Industrial Development Finance Limited, 4
Management of client enterprises:
  participation in, 56–58
  relations with, 49–58
Managers:
  qualifications of, 56, 58
  See also Staff
Margin:
  average, determinants of, 88–90
  of risk, 9
Market stabilization, 34, 43–45
Marketing of securities:
  controls in, 31, 35–37
  widening of, 39–42
Minority shareholders, 38
Monopoly position:
  of finance companies, 16, 17
Morocco, 2
Mutual funds, 41–42

Net defaults, 71
Net profits:
  percentage retained, 77
Net worth:
  and borrowing limits, 62
  and equity investments, 46
  and retained earnings, 77
Nigeria, 2
Nigerian Industrial Development Bank, 25, 37, 45

Objectives. *See* Goals
Opposition:
  to changes in business practices, 32, 37
Orientation:
  variations in, 11
Ownership of shares:
  expansion of, 25–47
  by finance company, 18, 38, 41
  local control of, 32, 37
  through public issues, 37–39, 40

Package sales:
  of securities, 42–43
Pakistan, 2, 3, 45
Pakistan Industrial Credit and Investment Corporation, 2, 4, 6, 37
Partners:
  functions of, 19–20
Passive role:
  of companies, 11
Pay-out ratio:
  guidelines for, 81–83
Personal relations:
  between directors and managers, 54
Personnel. *See* Staff
Philippines, 2, 39
Planning:
  governmental, 20, 94–96
Political pressures:
  effects of, 91, 100–2
Pool of securities:
  maintenance of, 45
Portfolio of company:
  development of, 38, 41, 73
  equity holdings in, 46
  government assistance to, 96
  provision for losses in, 79
  reduction of risks in, 84
  sales out of, 42–43
  taxation affecting, 87
Prestige projects:
  financing of, 104

Pricing:
  determination of, 42–43, 73
  stabilization of, 43–45
  and underwriting, 40–41
Priorities:
  in government planning, 94, 95
Private Development Corporation of the Philippines, 39
Private enterprise. *See* Business practices; Entrepreneurs
Private investors:
  securing confidence of, 36, 38, 39, 43, 81
Problems of financial policy, 59–90
Profitability:
  factors affecting, 29, 44, 59, 63, 65, 82, 83, 88–90
  and taxation, 86–87
Project:
  appraisal of, 9, 49, 52, 72
  development of, 8–9
  follow-up of, 53–54
  See also Feasibility studies
Promotion company, 16
Promotional activities:
  attitudes toward, 11, 18
  cost of, 15, 21–22
  cyclical movement in, 17
  factors in, 5–23, 38, 57, 107
  methods in, 17–20
  necessity for, 16–17
  over-involvement in, 20–21, 23
  requisites for, 20–21
  risks in, 20–23
  variations in, 10–11
Prospectus:
  preparation of, 39
Protective reserves:
  provision of, 77
Provisions:
  for possible losses, 77, 78–79
Public agencies:
  relationship with, 93, 103–6
  See also Government
Public issues:
  on best efforts basis, 39, 41
  need for, 37–38, 39, 40
  risks in, 23

Rate structure:
  government policies for 88–89, 97–98
Recessions:
  effects of, 71, 74
Regulations in marketing:
  development of, 40

Relationships:
  with governments, 91–107
  with management, 49–58
Reporting of information, 53–54, 55, 100, 102–3
Research:
  funds for, 15, 22
Reserves:
  establishment of, 60, 76–84
  on protection against losses, 77, 78–79
  and retention of earnings, 77, 79–84
  types of, 76–78
Resources:
  expansion of, 25–47, 63
Responsibilities:
  of bankers, 7–8
  of development finance companies, 44, 49, 91
  of financial institutions, 55, 56
  of World Bank Group, 70
Restrictions:
  in marketing, 40
  on retained earnings used, 83–84
  in risks, 22–23
Retention of earnings, 77, 79–84, 87
Return on investment, 29–30
Risk:
  basic parameters of, 74
  equity investments, 22–23
  evaluation of, 64, 65, 70, 73–75
  factors in, 72–73
  funds for coverage of, 77, 78–79
  government attitudes toward, 99, 100
  margin of, 9
  in price stabilization, 44
  in promotional activities, 20–23
  restrictions in, 22–23
  in underwriting, 40

Savings:
  investment possibilities for, 27, 28
  national, 33
Securities:
  expansion of ownership of, 25–47
  government, 31
  market stabilization for, 34, 43–45
  marketplace for, 29, 31, 34, 35–37
Security on loans, 35
  requirements for, 9, 52, 72
  types of, 29–30
Selection of investment proposals, 49, 52

Service to clients:
  importance of, 18
Shareholders. *See* Investors
Size of market:
  variations in, 43–44
Small groups:
  as businessmen, 51
Spain, 2, 3, 66, 87
Speculation:
  effects of, 36
Stabilization of market, 34, 43–45
Staff:
  on boards of client enterprises, 50, 54–56
  competence of, 72, 105
  costs of, 21
  effective use of, 17
  government attitudes toward, 95
  influence of, 29
  involvement of. *See* Involvement
  recruitment and training of, 11
  requisites for, 20
  specialized in marketing, 40
Stock exchanges, 31, 35–37
Study funds, 15, 22
Subordinated loans:
  aspects of, 62, 66–70, 80–81, 96, 99
  lender's view of, 67
  predomination of, 69–70
  problems of maturity, 67–69
  shareholder's view of, 66
Subsidies provided, 63, 67, 83, 104
Surveys. *See* Feasibility studies

Taiwan, 85
Taxation:
  on capital gains, 31, 87
  effects of, 30–31, 60, 77–79, 81, 86–88, 97
  and operations, 87–88
  and profitability, 86–87
  types of, 85
Technical assistance:
  from government, 96
Thailand, 3, 85
Tight money:
  effects of, 30
Trading mechanisms:
  development of, 31, 34, 35–37
Training:
  of dealers in securities, 40
Trusteeship:
  complications in, 35
Trusts:
  unit, 41–42
Turkey, 2, 70

Underdeveloped regions:
  governmental aid to, 99
Underwriting:
  aspects of, 19, 20, 39, 40–41, 89
  extent of, 45–46
  fees for, 41
Uneconomic projects:
  financing of, 104
Unit trusts, 41–42

Variations:
  in business practices, 10, 11, 14, 16, 51
  in capital structure, 62
  in ethics, 31–32
  in objectives, 62–63
  in orientation and approach, 11
  in promotional activities, 10–11
  in size of market, 43–44
Venezuela, 2, 66

Wealth:
  distribution of, 28
World Bank Group, 1, 70
Write-offs, 74, 78

Yields on investments. *See* Profitability

THE JOHNS HOPKINS PRESS

Designed by Gerard A. Valerio

Composed in Century Expanded by Monotype Composition Company

Printed Offset by Murray Printing Company on P & S, R

Bound by Murray Printing Company

DATE DUE

DEC 5 '72			
FEB 16 '79			
DE 04 '92			
NO 04 '05			
GAYLORD			PRINTED IN U.S.A.